1970

3 0301 00030755 9

This book may be kept

FN DAYS

Pope's Couplet Art

Pope's Couplet Art

John A. Jones

OHIO UNIVERSITY PRESS
Athens, Ohio
1969

Copyright © 1969 by John A. Jones

Library of Congress Catalog Number: 68–20932

Manufactured in the United States of America
by Kingsport Press, Inc., Kingsport, Tennessee

All rights reserved.

821.53
J754

This book is dedicated to

Bettina Jones and Hazel Jones Eidson

LIBRARY
College of St. Francis
JOLIET, ILL.

5 1591

Acknowledgments

I am more grateful than I can say to Aubrey Williams for his time and energy in reading and criticizing the manuscript of this study. I am proud of the encouragement of such a man, teacher, and scholar; but the faults of this study are wholly mine. I am indebted to Professor T. Walter Herbert for some penetrating observations on Pope's couplets. The Ohio University Research Committee aided me in the summer of 1967 with a grant which enabled me to give my time to finishing this study. Mr. Ian MacKenzie, Director of The Ohio University Press, has been helpful and generous with his time. I wish to thank also Mrs. Susan Schulman for help in preparing the manuscript. I thank the Shipley Art Gallery, Gateshead, England, for permission to reproduce the bust of Alexander Pope on the dust cover.

Table of Contents

1

❧

Introduction

EVEN A disciplined reader may feel a vague sense of bafflement when he seriously confronts Pope's couplet, especially if he reads an early and late poem in quick succession—the *Essay on Criticism* and the *Second Epistle of the Second Book of Horace*, for example. Although writing in the most rigid measure, Pope may seem too protean in his different impacts to be apprehended. He was clearly an "illusionist" with his couplets despite Matthew Arnold's placing him with Dryden as "classics of our prose," and Lord Macaulay's scornful dismissal of the Popean couplet as a measure that anyone could write. In both the early and late poems Pope seems to write in a similar style. Each group has neat, closed couplets, frequently with balanced hemistichs in one line, and the use of the rhyme is often similar. The graceful handling of the medial caesura is common to both, and on each side of the caesura is a slightly varied pacing of accented and unaccented syllables. Throughout Pope's best work a careful weighting and coloring of vowels is keyed and emphasized by consonant patterns too complex for systematic description. Yet one may have a troubled sense that in some way, not quickly or

easily apparent, the couplets of the early and late poems
are distinctly dissimilar and that the writer of the late
poems has undergone a subtle change of poetic view-
point and stylistic development. Prosodic analysis can tell us much about Pope's couplet art, and has;[1] yet because of our present inadequate
knowledge about the relation of sound to meaning, prosodic studies usually describe too much and explain too
little. There are other specialized disciplines that can no
doubt explain much about Pope's manipulation of language, particularly structural and descriptive linguistics.
But since the science of linguistics has so far not dealt
widely or deeply with the relation of language to literary
form and meaning, I have thought it useful at this point
in the continuing study of Pope to take the obvious and
basic features of Pope's couplet—balanced antithesis and
parallelism, rhyme, closure, and sentence form—and
consider how all these work together to create distinctive
modes of expression in different poems.

Readers do not take seriously any longer the Romantic
and Victorian attitude that Pope's verse is too clever and
intellectual to be real poetry. Because of several fine
studies his couplet is no longer thought a neoclassic iron
mold into which he elegantly cramped everything he
wrote about; and his magnificent skill and sensitivity in
the couplet is now more widely and significantly appre-
ciated than ever before. So I should explain my depend-
ence on some of these studies because of their value for
an understanding of Pope's verse. They have helped by
adumbrating principles of couplet structure and design
that I think indispensable for a fuller understanding of
Pope's art. In some instances, however, they omit principles which seem to me to require stressing.

Most historians of the neoclassic couplet have found in Pope's verse a brilliant culmination of the balance and parallelism developed by seventeenth-century couplet poets. In a basic study Ruth Wallerstein has shown how the line structure of the couplet moved from an unrelated or accidental balance between meter and sense in the early seventeenth century to the more graceful and precise structures of the later poets, who systematically began to exploit the possibilities of the couplet both for the balance of sense and idea, as well as that of meter and syntax.[2] This development was integral to what George Williamson in another basic study called the "rhetorical pattern of neoclassic wit," a pattern that comprehends the use of the sententious figures of inversion (antimetabole), antithesis (antitheton), and parallelism and balance (parison). Williamson found the main line of descent of the couplet's rhetorical development in Jonson, Waller, and especially in Dryden who brought the rhetoric of the couplet to the highest conciseness and discipline.[3] Of this general development Williamson wrote:

> As the Elizabethan quibble on words passed into the Metaphysical quibble on sense, so the latter passed into a new style of wit which depended less upon the ambiguity than upon the antithesis of ideas, or less upon startling reconciliations and more upon surprising oppositions. From the surprising opposition of ideas wit passed into verse as oppositions of structure.[4]

Thus, according to Wallerstein and Williamson, the couplet's capacity for pointed balance was developed and accelerated by Dryden and climaxed by Pope. In general this is a true account of the couplet's development, but it tends to overemphasize balance, which in this case is antithesis of structure and idea, at the expense of other features of the couplet form.

For example, if Denham and Waller, two main developers of the neoclassic couplet, are compared with Dryden and Pope, it will be strikingly clear that most of the verse of Dryden and Pope not only surpasses the work of the earlier masters in concise balance and parallelism but also in clear and graceful subordination. Dryden and Pope write effective sentences in the couplet form, and they form several couplets into the forceful verse paragraph of coherent artistic effect. They can fit a dazzling variety of long and short sentences into the rhyming iambic pentameter line so that both sentence and couplet emerge concisely and naturally.

Denham and Waller, except in the small amount of their good couplet poetry, consistently write awkward lines. Caesural division is uncertainly handled: the sense and syntax of the sentence generally seem either to limp behind or vault in front of the meter and rhyme, and phrases and clauses aimlessly straddle the end of the line. As a result, rhyming is often weak and hesitant or harsh and awkward. These weaknesses are related, of course, to the slowly developing balance and parallelism, prosodic and rhetorical, traced by Wallerstein and Williamson. Most of the earlier couplet poetry of Denham and Waller is consistently ineffective and clumsy, not only because they could not manage concise parallelism and balanced antithesis, but because they were still inept in the practice of the whole couplet form. While this study does not deal with the development of the couplet, I emphasize here that almost all of the couplet's structural possibilities reached their climax in the art of Dryden and Pope. Thus, I try to place Pope's balance and parallelism in an historical perspective that includes all the main structural features from which he developed his unique couplet style.

But the precise balance of the couplet, as everyone truly recognizes, is a touchstone of Pope's skill. Geoffrey Tillotson in *On the Poetry of Pope* has ably examined Pope's technique of balanced parallelism. Tillotson shows that Pope's use of balance is complex and varied because the poet balances and yokes phrases and ideas into parallelism at various positions in the line, or in different positions in a sentence that may extend through more than one couplet. The results of his mastery of balance are shadings of degrees of emphasis and contrast. He can achieve such effects not only by a neat balance of hemistich against hemistich but frequently by an asymmetrical imbalance.[5] The use of asymmetry refutes the assumption so often made that the main characteristic of Pope's parallelism is exactly this balance of hemistich against hemistich, or even of line against line. Tillotson's treatment of balance and line structure is invaluable because it helped destroy the assumption that Pope's couplets are monotonous in form as well as in meter, and it opened the way for a more varied response to Pope's sensitive use of balance. With Tillotson's aid, I hope to show that Pope uses balance in a thematic sense that goes beyond mere oppositions of structure within the couplets. Pope's use of balance varies; some poems require it and some do not. In his most successful works balance is used in contrast with relatively neutral forms of imbalance or with differently structured couplets that use no balance at all. Indeed, toward the end of his career Pope moved to a style that used sparingly the sharply paralleled half lines and witty antithesis characteristic of earlier works such as *An Essay on Criticism* and *The Rape of the Lock.*

The relationship between Pope's balance and parallelism and his rhyme is significant and interesting, and there is no more provocative analysis than that of W. K. Wimsatt, Jr. "One Relation of Rhyme to Reason" explains Pope's technique in making witty rhymes; of rhyme in the abstract Wimsatt writes:

> The words of a rhyme, with their curious harmony of sound and distinction of sense, are an amalgam of the sensory and the logical, or an arrest and precipitation of the logical in sensory form; they are the icon in which the idea is caught.[6]

In constructing his distinctive amalgams, Pope frequently rhymes words whose effect depends upon some clever or shocking disparity in meaning. The alogical relation of the rhymes creates simultaneously an ironic resemblance or difference between the rhyme words. This resemblance of sound plus the contrast or difference of meaning is emphasized by Pope's use of different parts of speech to achieve his rhymes. The two-fold relationship of the rhyme words gains in richness because of Pope's fondness for the use of antithetic parallels.[7] Wimsatt's comment is crucial:

> Pope's couplets, no matter what their syntax, tend to hover on the verge of antithesis and hence to throw a stress upon whatever difference of meaning appears in the rhyme words.[8]

For his analysis he cites such couplets as these:

> Whether the nymph shall break Diana's law
> Or some frail China jar receive a flaw.

> Thus Critics, of less *Judgement* than *Caprice,*
> *Curious,* not *Knowing,* not *exact,* but *nice.*

And of the chiastic reversal in these couplets he writes:

> In the first line the breakage, the fragile thing (the law);
> in the second line another fragile thing (the jar) and
> then its breaking (the flaw). The parallel is given a kind
> of roundness and completeness; the intellectual lines are
> softened into the concrete harmony of "law" and
> "flaw." The meaning is locked in a pattern of
> inevitability.[9]

> In the last example the antithesis is tripled, and the
> order being sufficiently chiastic, returns upon itself,
> which is sufficient complication to make "caprice" and
> "nice" a surprise. Then one is an adjective and one a
> noun, and "caprice" has two syllables.[10]

Wimsatt's analysis suggests the complexity of Pope's rhyming technique. But it should be emphasized that a great number of Pope's rhymes are neutral, as Wimsatt admits. It is doubtful however that "Pope's couplets, no matter what their syntax, tend to hover on the verge of antithesis." In many cases the second line adds to the meaning of the first, qualifying and complementing without suggesting antithesis. The following are typical of a great number of couplets where the rhymes are related in a consonant or agreeing manner rather than antithetically:

> Has God, thou fool! work'd solely for thy good,
> Thy joy, thy pastime, thy attire, thy food?

> The link dissolves, each seeks a fresh embrace,
> Another love succeeds, another race.
> (*Essay on Man*, III, 27–28, 129–30)[11]

"Food" is a complement and a part of "good"; "embrace" literally causes "race." The rhymes here give roundness and completeness to the parallels; the meaning is "locked in a pattern of inevitability," but not

antithetically, and the tight cross-reference of the rhyme
reinforces the logical and discursive meaning of the couplets. At least half of Pope's couplets are similar to these
because a large number are used for narration, exposition, and for purposes other than antithetical wit. For
example, Pope gives us a glimpse of the sleeping Belinda
in the opening of the *Rape of the Lock*:

> Thrice rung the Bell, the Slipper knock'd the Ground,
> And the press'd Watch return'd a silver Sound.
> *Belinda* still her downy Pillow prest,
> Her Guardian *Sylph* prolonged the balmy Rest.
>
> (Canto I, 17–20)

The subtle differences of meaning in the rhyme words
here are quite a different thing from the complicated
play of oblique wit in the couplets Wimsatt has discussed.

In one of the finest essays on Pope's poetry, Maynard
Mack has explained how Pope achieves poetic effects
without using metaphor in the distinctive way the Meta-
physicals used it; and Mack's summary opens up the
poetic technique of Pope's couplet to several kinds of
examination:

> I have tried to suggest that Pope is poetic, but not in the
> way the Metaphysicals are poetic, even where he is most
> like them; that if the prominent metaphor is the distinc-
> tive item in the practice of the Metaphysical poets, it
> has been replaced in Pope's poetry partly by devices of
> greater compression, like allusion and pun, partly by
> devices that are more distributive, like irony and mock-
> heroic, and of course by a multitude of other elements
> —the net effect of all these being to submerge the
> multiplicities of poetic language just beneath the single-
> ness of prose.[12]

One implication in Mack's summary is that in the hands
of Pope, the most gifted of rhymers, rhyme often empha-

sizes or supports several of the devices Mack mentions; and in Pope's best work rhyme is a manifestation of both form and content, of matter and manner. Mack's and Wimsatt's analyses merge at this point. Wimsatt makes clear that Pope's rhymes, when they are integral to his parallelism, achieve an ambience of contrasts of meaning, an ambience of different angles of analysis within the couplet. The effect is, to borrow Mack's words, "to submerge the multiplicities of poetic language just beneath the singleness of prose." It is true too that rhyme helps give proselike conciseness and formal, self-contained completeness to the couplet; but Pope's rhymes have a singular power of suggesting irony and complex wit which pulls against the "singleness of prose," and they imply, as well as submerge, the "multiplicities of poetic language."

The following couplets will show how Wimsatt's examination of rhyme and parallelism is related to Mack's view that Pope's poetic qualities lie just under the surface of the proselike characteristics of the couplet. The first is from a section of the *Essay on Man*, in which Pope's theme centers on the idea that emotion or passion always complicates and confuses the work of reason. The subject of the couplet is Newton:

> Could he, whose rules the rapid Comet bind,
> Describe or fix one movement of his mind?
>
> (II, 35–36)

Newton did not bind the comets within his law; he merely described their behavior, and "bind" is actually a metaphor for the power of the human mind to reach for infinite understanding. The first rhyme word does not really complete its meaning until it is given "roundness and completeness" by the second. Newton could not, of

course, describe or fix the movements of his mind, and
the word "bind" is used with a slight though doubled
irony. Pope can in one couplet pay homage to Newton,
marveling at the powers of his mind but in an ironic
sense, for the mind that can presumptuously bind the
stars can bind itself least of all.

This next couplet creates a more complicated poetry:

> Riches, like insects, when conceal'd they lie,
> Wait but for wings, and in their season, fly.
>
> (*Epistle to Bathurst*, 171–72)

It requires the perspective of the whole poem to show
the richness of this couplet. The wings awaited by this
dormant insect, gold, are paper money and paper credit.
Gold, insectlike, then flies over the earth, working mischief as often as it works good (paper money is like the
Sibyl's leaves flying on the wind, a figure which Pope has
developed earlier in the poem). There is also the power
of pun in "lie"; for riches tempt and betray, and like an
insect, their season is often brief and disastrous. So when
riches "fly," when gold is winged (or "imp'd" by paper
credit, as Pope has said earlier), it can "lie" in another
sense than to lie dormant in the earth. In spite of the
concise, almost aphoristic quality of these couplets, the
character of the rhyme, the allusions to his developing
context, and the irony create a tension between the singleness of prose and the multiple powers of poetic language. This tension is one of the most interesting features of Pope's poetry, and I try to take account of it
whenever it seems significant.

Pope uses the individual couplet and its balance and
rhyme for various concentrated effects. But his genius
lies also in composing the passage and the verse para-

graph, a leading way of transcending the couplet's brief
and rigid form. R. K. Root points out:

> When Pope's metrical art is at its best, his couplets do
> not merely follow one upon another's heels. They group
> themselves into the larger unit of the verse-paragraph,
> the group being held together both by the logic of the
> sense and by the cadence of the modulation. This is
> particularly true of his more impassioned poetry—the
> elevated eloquence of the *Essay on Man* or the intense
> scorn of his great satire.[13]

Root asserts here an organic principle of continuity as
well as differentiation in Pope's verse paragraphs; and as
in Tillotson's treatment of Pope's parallelism, the assumption that Pope's couplets are monotonously structured received a well-deserved setback. By implication
Root undermines another widely held assumption that
most of Pope's couplets are closed, and a correlative but
false assumption that they are also end-stopped. Root's
perception that Pope's paragraphs have a "cadence of
. . . modulation" is significant; and in this study I frequently examine Pope's structural modifications of his
couplets in passages and paragraphs. Often he employs
several suspended or open couplets, and the effect is
frequently climactic because of the concentration of the
passage and because of the contrast with closed couplets.
The structural design, the modulation of structure and
sense in Pope's individual passages as he may move from
antithesis and parallelism through complex neutral structures to asymmetrical parallelism, is a technique that can
tell us much about the variety as well as the development
of his style.

Earlier studies have given us most of the basic techniques for a study of the characteristics of Pope's style;

and in discussing the poems, I attempt to use these studies directly and to adapt their methods and conclusions. A most significant aspect of Pope's stylistic art is his use of a "couplet norm" or dominant style for each poem. (I mean about the same thing by norm and dominant style except that style is a larger and more inclusive term, while norm is slightly more definite and concrete.) When many of the couplets in a poem employ similar syntactic patterns, when these same patterns recur frequently throughout the poem, and when they carry the main theme or meaning, we have a couplet norm for the poem. Such couplet norms vary from poem to poem. In one poem this norm may be a couplet with balanced antithesis in one of its lines; in a second poem it may be a sentence of compound clauses or predicates; in another it may be a sentence or closed couplet of simple straightforward syntax, however varied; and in still another the couplet norm may have a rugged, irregular structure and syntax. In some poems Pope's couplet structure is so varied that he cannot be said to employ a couplet norm at all. When this occurs, he achieves a particular style for the poem through the structures of the individual couplets taken as a whole, and through the domination of the poem by passages and paragraphs of distinctive designs. The couplet norm or dominant style of a poem derives its identity, therefore, from the sentence form and line structure of the couplet; but in Pope's poetry, line structure and sentence form are not meaningful if they are separated from balance and parallelism, rhyme, end-stopping, and closure. All of these features working together in a distinctive way create couplet norm and dominant style as well as variations on the norm, so I shall examine the bearing of all upon a poem, but with varying frequency and emphasis, since this is how Pope himself used them from poem to poem.

This pattern of norm and variation is complex and subtle and does not neatly or simply explain the style of a poem. When more than half of a poem's couplets have similar structures, and when this "couplet majority" expresses the main theme and meaning of the poem, we have a clearly perceived couplet norm. But Pope is more elusive than this. For example, slightly over half of the couplets of *An Essay on Criticism* are not balanced, but balanced lines are used so frequently and consistently to express the main themes that balance is obviously the couplet norm of the poem. Whether or not this couplet majority is the couplet norm must depend, therefore, upon the character of the poem and upon Pope's strategy of emphasis, although the couplet norm or dominant style always comprises a greater number of a poem's couplets than does any type of stylistic variation.

The task of this study therefore is threefold: (1) to show how and for what thematic and artistic reasons Pope employs different couplet norms for different poems, and if a couplet norm is not discernible, to account for the stylistic mode of the poem, whatever it is; (2) to explain Pope's development as a stylist; (3) and, finally, to offer some tentative conclusions about the nature and significance of Pope's art as a couplet poet. But I do not attempt to explain, because I do not find, a total configuration or system in the whole of Pope's verse. Therefore, this study does not pretend to be a blueprint of Pope's art. I hope that it is, rather, a discovery and exploration of the dynamic patterns of Pope's couplet structure and design and of their relationship to his controlling poetic vision.

Ultimately Pope's use of changing couplet structures
and styles is an organic manifestation of meaning. I
therefore treat couplet structure or couplet style as the
reflection of the meaning of each poem. For many readers this attempt may bring up the question of exactly
how couplet structure or style reflects meaning. Could
not Pope have written *Windsor-Forest* in the style of the
Dunciad and created the same meaning, or the *Rape of
the Lock* in the style of the *Epilogue to the Satires?* If by
meaning we imply discursive philosophic meaning or
that which paraphrase yields, the answer is yes, and style
is a mere matter of ornamentation. But meaning is, of
course, an organic whole of content, point of view, rhetorical and metaphoric structure, and style. But style, or
couplet structure and design, cannot by itself reflect differences of meaning. What style reflects, and creates, is
the particular character and texture of the work, and
qualities of sensitivity and point of view through which
the writer reveals his feeling for his subject and the
character of his involvement as creator. So this study is
based upon a conception of meaning that is not at all
original, but one that emphasizes now and then other
aspects of meaning than the usual ones of complex or-
ganization of content and of metaphoric and rhetorical
structure. When I give an account of the meaning or
subject of a poem, I am not competing with those schol-
ars who have deepened and clarified our knowledge and
conception of Pope's philosophic, literary, or political
world, or who have given us definitive explications of his
poems. My purpose is not to increase our knowledge of
the poem's philosophic content, literary background, or
patterns of metaphor and allusion, but rather to set up
an accurate, generalized plot or core of the poem's mean-

ing in order to show how Pope's use of style is related to the central meaning or theme of the poem.

Pope's couplet art is more than a scintillating instrument of wit and elegance perfected in his youth and never modulated; it is subtle, flexible, and capable of different voices and manners. The contrast, for example, between *An Essay on Criticism* and the *Epilogue to the Satires* is radical; and the difference of couplet style is a reflection not only of difference of meaning, but of genre, of point of view or persona, and of poetic texture. I hope, therefore, that this study of the dynamic changes of Pope's couplet style in eight of his poems will bring us a richer and more varied insight into his poetry.

NOTES

1. I refer to Jacob H. Adler's recent study, *The Reach of Art: A Study in the Prosody of Pope* (Gainesville: University of Florida Press, 1964).

2. "The Development of the Rhetoric and Metre of the Heroic Couplet, Especially in 1625–1645," *Publications of the Modern Language Association*, L (1935), 166–209.

3. "The Rhetorical Pattern of Neoclassical Wit," *Modern Philology*, 33 (1935), 55–81.

4. *Ibid.*, pp. 74–75.

5. *On the Poetry of Pope* (Oxford: Oxford University Press, Inc., 1938), pp. 125–29.

6. *The Verbal Icon* (Lexington: University of Kentucky Press, 1954), p. 165.

7. *Ibid.*, pp. 153–66, *passim*.

8. *Ibid.*, p. 159.

9. *Ibid.*, p. 162.

10. *Ibid.*, p. 163.

11. All quotations from Pope's poems are from *The Twickenham Edition of the Poems of Alexander Pope* (7 Vols.), John Butt, General Editor (London: Methuen and Co. Ltd., and New Haven:

Yale University Press, 1940–1961.) This edition will be referred to here as *Twick. Ed.*

12. " 'Wit and Poetry and Pope': Some Observations on His Imagery," *Pope and His Contemporaries: Essays Presented to George Sherburn* (Oxford: Oxford University Press, 1949), p. 40.

13. *The Poetical Career of Alexander Pope* (Princeton, N.J.: Princeton University Press, 1938), pp. 46–47.

2

❦

The *Pastorals* 1709

It is interesting to see Pope mastering in so special a genre as the pastoral couplet structures that, with subtle changes, he was to use later with lasting effects. The *Pastorals* are often passed over as mere apprentice works or technical exercises; but it is worthwhile to examine briefly some of the main aspects of Pope's theory of pastoral in order to understand the conventions and in this case the special limitations under which he wrote. A writer's theory does not necessarily determine his practice, but in a clear though general way Pope's does. In *A Discourse on Pastoral Poetry* Pope defines pastoral loosely along the lines of Aristotelian imitation:

> A Pastoral is the imitation of the action of a shepherd, or one considered under that character. The form of this imitation is dramatic, or narrative, or mixed of both; the fable simple, the manners not too polite nor too rustic: The thoughts are plain, yet admit a little quickness and passion, but that short and flowing: The expression humble, yet as pure as the language will afford; neat, but not florid; easy and yet lively. In short, the fable, manners, thoughts, and expressions, are full of the greatest simplicity in nature.[1]

One notices immediately the crucial qualification that
pastoral is not necessarily the imitation of a real shepherd, but "one considered under that character," which
leaves the door of Aristotelian imitation slightly ajar; and
when Pope says that the fable, manners, thoughts, and
expression are "full of the greatest simplicity in nature,"
we can take it that "nature" is Pope's idealization and
summary of the pastoral tradition. About the verisimili-
tude and "realism" of nature in pastoral, Pope wrote
further:

> If we would copy Nature, it may be useful to take this
> idea along with us, that pastoral is an image of what
> they call the Golden age. So that we are not to describe
> our shepherds as shepherds at this day really are, but as
> they may be conceiv'd then to have been; when the best
> of men follow'd the employment.[2]

Pope makes it clear in the *Discourse* that his "Nature"
is that of previous writers of pastoral, especially Theocritus, Virgil, and Spenser, to whom he has made his bow
and who are the "good old authors" he has been careful
to imitate. In the poems themselves, he borrows, alludes
to, and refocuses materials from all of these while steer-
ing between the two dominant schools of pastoral influential in the late seventeenth and early eighteenth centu-
ries: the Golden Age view of René Rapin, and the
Rationalistic view of Bernard Le Bovier de Fontenelle.
Rapin, who derived his neoclassic theory from Virgil and
the critical writings of Aristotle and Horace, maintained
that pastoral should be an imitation of a shepherd living
in the Golden Age. As a result, according to Audra and
Williams:

> . . . a pastoral should reflect the innocence and peace
> of that age and the virtues and simplicity of the shep-

herds who lived in it; because shepherds in this ancient past were often princes or men of affairs, the characters and language should be simple and pure rather than "clownish"; the scene should be simple and decorous, as in Virgil; the matter should reflect only the simple affairs of shepherds, that is, the loves and sorrows of a simple rural life; the fable should be simple and plain, the style neat and plain.[3]

Fontenelle, on the other hand, thought a pastoral should represent the leisure and tranquillity of a shepherd's life varied with the passion most congenial to the indolence of man's nature—love. Thus, the writer of pastoral should conceal the misery and meanness of the pastoral life and show only its innocence and pleasantness. Pope preferred the view of Rapin, yet employed Fontenelle's "pleasure principle" too. But as Audra and Williams point out, the two schools differed mainly in the sources from which each sought its ultimate authority; and pastoral written according to the principles of one could possibly be like a pastoral written according to the other. Pope incorporates in the following passage Fontenelle's principles, and also gets to the heart of his own practice:

We must therefore use some illusion to render a Pastoral delightful; and this consists in exposing the best side only of a shepherd's life, and in concealing its miseries. Nor is it enough to introduce shepherds discoursing together in a natural way; but a regard must be had to the subject; that it contain some particular beauty in itself, and that it be different in every Eclogue. Besides, in each of them a design'd scene or prospect is to be presented to our view, which should likewise have its variety. This Variety is obtain'd in a great degree by frequent comparisons, drawn from the most agreeable objects of the country; by interrogations to things inanimate; by beautiful digressions, but those short; sometimes by insisting a little on circumstances; and lastly by elegant turns on the words, which render the numbers extremely sweet and pleasing. As for the numbers themselves, tho' they are properly of the heroic measure, they should be the smoothest, the most easy and flowing imaginable.[4]

Pope expresses three principles here that are important for understanding the nature of his achievement in the *Pastorals*. First, he does not mean to deliberately falsify the pastoral life but to idealize or transcend it; and his poems go beyond his bald statement of "exposing the best side only of a shepherd's life." He suppresses the everyday realism of the pastoral life, but not the simple griefs and passions that all men share, whether shepherds or kings. Second, Pope's illusion of delight is to be achieved by variety among the eclogues and in each eclogue itself. The pattern of variety that Pope employs in the poems themselves is rather superficial and stiff; but he does not forget, as we shall see, that each poem should have a particular beauty. Third, variety as well as delight are to be achieved by language and versification, both of which are to be simple and flowing but neat and elegant. The term "elegant" jars slightly in this context, but "elegance" can well be a quality of shepherds who are under no necessity to be real.

The *Pastorals* are ultimately an interpretation in Pope's own terms of a genre that had been in many respects stylized and conventional for a long time. As Pope well knew, his Golden Age shepherds, those "best of men," were creatures of his imagination—an imagination held in check by a "judgment" steeped in the literature of the pastoral tradition. But if Pope achieved what he intended—the objectification of his theory of pastoral, and a convincing display of his early artistry—he managed to write a work that is only up to a certain point described and explained by his theory. We pass from the innocent exuberance of *Spring* through the slightly ironic introspection in *Summer* and the melancholy lament of *Autumn* to the removal of the shepherds at the end of *Winter* from the pastoral outdoors to seek warmth, for "Nature feels decay." Admittedly the emotion of this progression is neither deep nor charged with the dramatic; but there is enough contrast between the desires of the shepherds and the inexorable revolutions of time and nature to suggest at least a slight degree of movement and tension.[5] The formal roundness and completeness of the *Pastorals* suggest, "in little," the idealized world picture held by the Augustans, but the picture Pope gives us is not wholly pretty or complacent; it is one of acceptance of misfortune and disappointment as a part of the natural course of things. Pope's Augustan shepherds must face age-old problems even if they face them in simplified and generalized ways; and if they are only Augustan beaux or coffeehouse wits playing at being swains, they play the game with a sense that they are a part of the nature in which they act.

II

The style of the *Pastorals* is basically straightforward and simple. If the couplets of the four poems are taken altogether, one finds that between a third and a fourth of the couplets are unpatterned:

Now rise, and haste to yonder Woodbine Bow'rs,
A soft Retreat from sudden vernal Show'rs.
(*Spring*, 97–98)

Accept the Wreath which You deserve alone,
In whom all Beauties are compriz'd in One.
(*Summer*, 57–58)

Now blushing Berries paint the Yellow Grove;
Just Gods! shall all things yield Returns but Love?
(*Autumn*, 75–76)

Thyrsis, the Musick of that murm'ring Spring
Is not so mournful as the Strains you sing.
(*Winter*, 1–2)

We find a variety of sentence forms, and the unit of
construction is not the half line but the whole line. The
grammar and syntax are almost that of ordinary prose.
The sentences, however, are just a little stiff, formal, and
wasteful. Later on Pope's syntax shows greater ruggedness and compression than "In whom all Beauties are
compriz'd in One," and "Is not so mournful as the
Strains you sing." The point, however, is that in the
unpatterned couplets, Pope was trying to work a simple
syntax and sentence form into neat couplets. He was also
learning to master balance and parallelism: his frequent
use of the compound sentence sharply divided by the
two lines of the couplet, and of doubled sentence parts
such as predicates and simple subordinate clauses, makes
parallelism heavily dominant in the *Pastorals*. The following examples are typical of the couplet norm:

Here the bright Crocus and blue Vi'let glow;
Here Western Winds on breathing Roses blow.
(*Spring*, 31–32)

Let op'ning Roses knotted Oaks adorn,
And liquid Amber drop from ev'ry Thorn.
(*Autumn*, 37–38)

The Garlands fade, the Vows are worn away;
So dies her Love, and so my Hopes decay.
(*Autumn*, 69–70)

But see, *Orion* sheds unwholesome Dews,
Arise, the Pines a noxious Shade diffuse.

(Winter, 85–86)

Adjective-noun pairs like "breathing Roses" and "liquid Amber" abound in the *Pastorals*; and, when carried by the simple parallelism of the first two couplets, quickly grow tiresome. Pope seems to be striving for richness of texture and the inadvertent result is thinness of meaning; two pairs in a line take up too many of the ten syllables, there is not much left to work with, the lines lose their forward movement and grow static and decorative.

In these simple parallels, however, Pope was developing two principles of couplet structure: rhyming and interplay of meaning between parallel statements within the couplet. In the first couplet the inversion puts the verb in rhyme position and creates an ambient activity of "glowing" and "blowing." We do not need to be told—the parallels and the rhymes suggest it for us—that roses do not adorn thorns, they adorn oaks; but the parallel vertical binding of the rhymes along with a reversal of verb and object suggest that "liquid Amber" is an adornment of "Thorn." The statements in each of the last two couplets are paralleled in similar syntax. Perhaps the cause-effect relations between the parallels is a little obvious; but the criss-cross vertical relations of the meaning as well as the horizontal relations point toward the complex parallelism of the later Pope. The brilliant effects with rhyme and parallelism characteristic of Pope in his maturity are just slightly adumbrated here. Pope could not have his Golden Age shepherds speaking couplets of complex wit, although occasionally he allows them some figures of rhetoric and some rather tricky effects with balance, as we shall see in a moment.

The couplet styles of the four poems, while not as

effectively related to the themes as in Pope's later works, do their part in supporting Pope's aim of having a particular beauty in each eclogue. In each eclogue the simpler type of compounding parallelism, in which one statement is added to another, is slightly varied because a different theme creates a slightly different massing and design of the couplets. In *Spring* the competing scheme of the singing match is rounded out in a strictly balanced fashion reflected in the individual couplets and in their grouping. After answering each other in paragraphs of three couplets each, the shepherds settle down in the contest itself to exchanges of two couplets, in which the nymph of each shepherd is praised in terms of her resemblance to the vernal surrounding, or the emotions aroused by love are equated with natural occurrences within the pastoral world:

STREPHON
All Nature mourns, the Skies relent in Show'rs,
Hush'd are the Birds, and clos'd the drooping Flow'rs;
If *Delia* smile, the Flow'rs begin to spring,
The Skies to brighten, and the Birds to sing.

DAPHNIS
All Nature laughs, the Groves are fresh and fair,
The Sun's mild Lustre warms the vital Air;
If *Sylvia* smiles, new Glories gild the Shore,
And vanquish'd Nature seems to charm no more.
(*Spring*, 69–76)

Each shepherd attempts to outdo the other while using a similar couplet design. Although Pope employs designs more varied than this one, yet the couplets of *Spring* are the simplest and the most rigidly patterned he ever wrote. Pope holds an even tighter rein in *Spring* than in the other poems and seems on the whole too careful, afraid to modulate his dominant design at all. But here is a better passage:

> Soon as the Flocks shook off the nightly Dews,
> Two Swains, whom Love kept wakeful, and the Muse,
> Pour'd o'er the whitening Vale their fleecy Care,
> Fresh as the Morn, and as the Season fair.
>
> (*Spring*, 17–20)

The careless ambiguity of "Muse" has been noted by several commentators. Geoffrey Tillotson's penetrating discussion of this passage shows how Pope combines old and new diction to create an original image. Pope takes old expressions from Virgil and Spenser, such as "nightly Dews," "whitening Vale," and "fleecy Care," and combines them with sharp, original perceptions—"shook off" and the unusual verb "pour'd" so that we get the striking freshness of the shepherd literally "pouring" his herd of sheep onto the field.[6] The design of the couplets aids this combination of the new and the old, and Pope uses a rhythmic pattern that alternates between broken and unbroken lines by contrasting lines 1 and 3 with lines 2 and 4. "Pour'd," the striking verb in the strong first position, sets the sweeping, unbroken line in motion. The last line pulls up the movement; and its chiasmus, with "fresh" and "fair" in the first and last positions, makes a sound pattern which flows from strong to weak to strong. Such a chiastically balanced emphasis gives a slight originality to the line rather than the triteness of the natural order, "fresh and fair." It is unfortunate that *Spring* does not have more passages like this, but the poem does have a kind of charm. In the quiet beauty of their surroundings, the shepherds take their sheep to the

LIBRARY
5/5/91 College of St. Francis
JOLIET. ILL

field and sing while a ploughman turns the ground with his oxen. At the end of the poem, they retire from the field to a grove to escape the spring shower. A very simple pattern, but there is enough involvement of the shepherds with their environment to keep the poem from becoming static. The simple, compound structures of the couplets just touched with the various lilts and rhythms of Pope's balance, chiasmus, and zeugma create in *Spring* a singing freshness in spite of its overuse of "poetic" pastoral diction.

Summer, a love complaint, has an acrid, introspective quality lacking in *Spring*. The love-bitten shepherd's basic mode of expression is that of comparison of his emotions with the world of nature which, in this case, is the sheep, the fields, and the weather; and though he finds surface similarities between his feelings and the conditions of nature, he usually discovers an underlying antithetic contrast. The defeating self-absorption of which he is a victim finds its most urgent expression in sharply balanced antithesis, the main variation within the *Pastorals* as a whole. The unhealthy mood of the poem is defined by this couplet which suggests that even in Pope's idyllic, golden world of pastoral, frailty and passion can now and then appear:[7]

> This harmless Grove no lurking Viper hides,
> But in my Breast the Serpent Love abides.
> > (*Summer*, 67–68)

After beginning the poem with a short description of Alexis leading forth his flock, Pope, with an antithetic, tongue-in-cheek flourish, dedicates *Summer* to his friend Garth:

Accept, O *Garth*, the Muse's early Lays,
That adds this Wreath of Ivy to thy Bays;
Hear what from Love unpractis'd Hearts endure,
From Love, the sole Disease thou canst not cure!
  Ye shady Beeches, and ye cooling Streams,
Defence from *Phoebus'*, not from *Cupid's* Beams . . .

(*Summer,* 9–12)

The recoiling second couplet further defines the theme
with the imbalanced repetition of "Love." The balanced
antithesis of the last line sets the pattern for much of the
love complaint in which disappointed love is compared
to the burning, drying heat of summer:

The bleating Sheep with my Complaints agree,
They parch'd with Heat, and I inflam'd by thee.

(*Summer,* 19–20)

The antithesis of this couplet, which contrasts the brute
sensation of the sheep to the desiccating mental heat of
the lover Alexis, is paralleled by a later one in which he
nicely reveals his "disease":

Then might my Voice thy list'ning Ears employ,
And I those Kisses he receives, enjoy.

(*Summer,* 47–48)

In the second line the displaced verb "enjoy" suddenly
pops up in rhyme position and emphasizes the active,
positive nature of the lover's desire in contrast with the
weak and passive way he wishes to imagine his successful
rival's enjoyment. The displacement, therefore, emphasizes the jealous imagination of the lover. "Receive" and
"enjoy" are juxtaposed to bring out the active-passive
reversal, here a technique of swift illumination. The line

also shows that Pope can flash an antithesis without the balanced hemistichs that is too frequently supposed to be its inevitable carrier.

Summer contains a famous passage, delightful in its own right, which Handel set to music in his oratorio *Semele:*

> Oh deign to visit our forsaken Seats,
> The mossie Fountains, and the Green Retreats!
> Where-e'er you walk, cool Gales shall fan the Glade,
> Trees, where you sit, shall crowd into a Shade,
> Where-e'er you tread, the blushing Flow'rs shall rise,
> And all things flourish where you turn your Eyes.
>
> (*Summer,* 71–76)

The passage is a marvel of the harmony of vowel assonance and contrast. Reuben A. Brower notes the rhythm of the passage as well as its structural units:

> Consider the variations in rhythm of the five numbered lines: first (71), the unbroken flow of 'Oh deign to visit our forsaken seats'; then (72) the exact balance of 'The mossie fountains, and the green retreats!', and (73) the asymmetrical balance of 'where'er you walk, // cool gales shall fan the glade'; the broken music of the following line (74) with an architectural triad of units increasing in length, 'Trees,// where you sit,/ shall crowd into a shade'; next (75), an almost exact renewal of 73 in 'Where'er you tread,/ the blushing flowers shall rise'; and finally the line (76) that ends this 'stanza,' which recalls the unbroken flow of the first (71) by the lack of any sharp pause, the many liquids, and the rich assonance: 'And all things flourish where you turn your eyes.'[8]

The dominant parallelism we have seen all along is used here, but with a varied flow and music as Brower makes clear. The main burden of the shepherd's complaint, however, is in contrast with this consonant parallelism; for this passage is a brief wish of the disappointed Alexis, and the nymph does not come.

The antithetical tendencies of *Summer* are rather fiercely and rhetorically summarized in the final flourish which ends the poem:

> But soon the Sun with milder Rays descends
> To the cool Ocean, where his Journey ends;
> On me Love's fiercer Flames for ever prey,
> By Night he scorches, as he burns by Day.
>
> (*Summer*, 89–92)

The fast, run-on first couplet is a suitable prelude for the sharp thrusts of the last line, where the lover continues to burn—appropriately in a chiastic balance. Alexis tends to be witty; and his fits of antithesis contrast with the more agreeing union with nature characteristic of the shepherds in *Spring, Autumn,* and *Winter*.

In *Autumn* Pope loosens up the rigid simplicity of the parallelism of *Spring*, and like the sun itself, if one may say so, moderates the antithesis of *Summer*. *Autumn* is based on the same alternate singing scheme as *Spring* but like *Summer* is a love complaint. One shepherd complains for an absent love, the other for a perjured love; and at the close the victim of perjury resolves to throw himself from a cliff. The formal exchanges of four and six lines of *Spring* are missing, and the lament of each extends through some thirty-odd lines. The characteristic design is a cumulative, anaphoral parallelism that contrasts with the more sharply demarked closed couplets of *Spring* and *Summer*. The *Pastorals* contain an overwhelming number of closed couplets, but *Autumn* has

the greatest number of incomplete ones which gives it a
greater rush and singing quality. Early in the poem Pope
breaks into an open series in the apostrophe to William
Wycherley, to whom he dedicated *Autumn:*

> Thou, whom the Nine with *Plautus'* Wit inspire,
> The Art of *Terence,* and *Menander's* Fire;
> Whose Sense instructs us, and whose Humour charms,
> Whose Judgment sways us, and whose Spirit warms!
> Oh, skill'd in Nature! see the Hearts of Swains,
> Their artless Passions, and their tender Pains.
>
> (*Autumn,* 7–12)

The parallels of the first couplet show us what the Muses
do to Wycherley, and the chiastic second line creates the
felicitous rhyme "inspire-Fire." Then the parallels veer
from what the Muses do to Wycherley to what Wycherley does to us. With the suppression of "us," "charms"
and "warms" emerge in rhyme position and make an
appropriate relation with the previous rhyme "inspire-
Fire." The parallels are much more symmetrical than
Pope liked to use later; but he at least maneuvers them
enough to change the direction of his phalanx and to
create with the relations of the first four rhyme words an
active, pleasing emotional aura for his introduction.

In the next passage the rigid caesuras of the passage to
Wycherley are varied better:

> Go gentle Gales, and bear my Sighs along!
> 2 The Birds shall cease to tune their Ev'ning Song,
> The Winds to breathe, the waving Woods to move,
> 4 And Streams to murmur, e'er I cease to love.
> Not bubling Fountains to the thirsty Swain,
> 6 Not balmy Sleep to Lab'rers faint with Pain,

> Not Show'rs to Larks, or Sunshine to the Bee,
> 8 Are half so charming as thy Sight to me.
>
> (*Autumn*, 39–46)

Here is one of the first examples of Pope's anaphoral parallels with sudden conclusions as in the second hemistich of line 4, and the longer sweep of the last line. Rhetorical though it is, the negative build-up of this passage will point for every reader of Pope to a passage in the *Rape of the Lock:*

> Not youthful Kings in Battel seiz'd alive,
> Not scornful Virgins who their Charms survive,
> Not ardent Lovers robb'd of all their Bliss,
> Not ancient Ladies when refus'd a Kiss,
> Not Tyrants fierce that unrepenting dye,
> Not *Cynthia* when her *Manteau's* pinn'd awry,
> E'er felt such Rage, Resentment, and Despair,
> As thou, sad Virgin! for thy ravish'd Hair.
>
> (Canto IV, 3–10)

The second passage reads like a parody of the first. It is not, of course, but Pope's shepherds were forming some techniques that they would use with devastating effects later on when they cast their quick eyes on the incongruities of Augustan society.

The next passage is perhaps the most original and certainly the most shapely in *Autumn:*

> Resound ye Hills, resound my mournful Strain!
> Of perjur'd *Doris*, dying I complain:
> Here where the *Mountains* less'ning as they rise,
> Lose the low Vales, and steal into the Skies.
> While the lab'ring Oxen, spent with Toil, and Heat,
> In their loose Traces from the *Field* retreat;

While curling Smokes from Village-Tops are seen,
And the fleet Shades glide o'er the dusky Green.
(Autumn, 56–64)

Pope circumvents the too regular closure and frequency of the simple declarative couplet by following the first couplet with three varied, subordinating completions. The subordinating couplets introduce one of his favorite techniques, the "where–while" construction that varies and prolongs the action or description by alternating the place–time direction of the couplets to achieve an effect of multiple activity or viewpoint. In the passage above it is not the descriptive power of the adjectives that makes the scene, but as is so often the case with Pope, the harmonious construction of the whole. The second couplet is an instance of the subtle harmony that Pope often employs to mold and shape a passage. The "less'ning" mountains "rise," "lose," and "steal." "Lose," in the strong first position, is a low vowel which literally falls from the higher vowel "rise," immediately preceding; and the low vowels are suddenly left behind. But the second half of the line "steals" upward again by way of the liquid continuant in "steal," back to the higher rhyme sound "Skies." The couplet structure and the sound quality create the visual quality of the mountains stealing distantly into the sky from the scene below. Pope makes a suggestive use of the verbs and verbals, "lab'ring," "spent," "retreat," "curling," and "glide," which, in characterizing the nouns, create a quiet idyllic scene with a kind of sealed- in, retreating activity. At first glance the passive "are seen" seems weak, but an active verb would require an active observer who would not be in key with the quiet scene.

The open parallels which are so noticeable a variation in *Autumn* yield to greater closure of the couplets in *Winter*; and missing is the symmetrical parallelism of *Spring* and the balanced antithesis of *Summer*. The couplets of *Winter* are a little quieter and straighter in structure, appropriately, since *Winter* is a eulogy for a dead shepherdess, and Pope touches up the scene in a fine couplet:

> Now sleeping Flocks on their soft Fleeces lye,
> The Moon, serene in Glory, mounts the Sky.
>
> (*Winter*, 5–6)

The couplet is not unusual or striking, but its structure carries a sound pattern as well as a kinetic pattern that shapes the scene. In the first line, the sibilants, the drawn-out assonance of "sleeping" and "Fleeces," and the alliteration of "Flocks" and "Fleeces," with their contrasting vowel sounds, suggest the softness and quietness of the action. The second line, with its double pause and with the verb and object emerging quickly but quietly, comes out effectively against the first. The verb "mounts" contrasts with the more inactive verb "lye" of the first line; and the action of the moon is nicely contrasted with the sleeping flocks. This couplet is typical of the best in the *Pastorals*; its effect is not sharply noticeable as in great poetry, but it evokes the quietness and serenity of a moonlit night.

Another good couplet but without the distinctive movement of the preceding one is the following:

> Behold the Groves that shine with silver Frost,
> Their Beauty wither'd, and their Verdure lost.
>
> (*Winter*, 9–10)

The majority of the couplets of the *Pastorals* are by no means this good; for example, we find this passage in *Winter*:

> No more the mounting Larks, while *Daphne* sings,
> Shall list'ning in mid Air suspend their Wings;
> No more the Birds shall imitate her Lays,
> Or hush'd with Wonder, hearken from the Sprays:
> No more the Streams their Murmurs shall forbear,
> A sweeter Musick than their own to hear,
> But tell the Reeds, and tell the vocal Shore,
> Fair *Daphne*'s dead, and Musick is no more!
>   (*Winter*, 53–60)

In spite of the good first couplet and the marvelous sound quality of this passage, it is rather decorative filler; even in Pope's day such an attribution of consciousness to things and animals was regarded as an affectation acceptable only in epic and pastoral where the author was imitating ancient models such as Homer and Virgil, and in this case, Theocritus. But the couplets are at least supple and straightforward, and the absence of the balanced pairs of trochaic adjectives and nouns is a relief. In *Winter*, unlike the other eclogues, Pope was just slightly moving toward greater spareness in his couplets.

The closing lines of *Winter* are Pope's adieu to the pastoral world and perhaps to the illusion that such an idyllic world could ever have existed anyway:

> But see *Orion* sheds unwholesome Dews,
> Arise, the Pines a noxious Shade diffuse;
> Sharp *Boreas* blows, and Nature feels Decay,
> Time conquers All, and We must Time obey.
>   (*Winter*, 85–88)

The second couplet contains in the first line a significant progression from concrete to general (from "Boreas" to

"Nature"); and in the second line, a deepening progression from "Time" to "All" to "We," then chiastically back to "Time" in the closing cadence "Time obey." The deepening of the parallels gives a hint of the mature Pope; and they are one of the instances in the *Pastorals* that go beyond Pope's theory that only the pleasant side of a shepherd's life should be shown.

III

Pope not only forged his basic technique of parallelism in his first work, but experimented with the figures of rhetoric. In the *Discourse on Pastoral*, he recommended "elegant turns on the words," meaning not only the use of the turn in a technical sense—that is, the figurative use of a word or of language in general—but apparently the use of all the figures. His handling of the figures and tropes in the *Pastorals* is rather obtrusive and decorative, but with age and experience he used them with greater ease and subtlety, and less frequently. It is interesting to see him trying some for the first time, and some for the last. For example, here is the *anadiplosis* or *reduplicato* (and if the reader has forgotten these terms, their meaning will be immediately clear, once the following passage is read):

> Her Fate is whisper'd by the gentle Breeze,
> And told in Sighs to all the trembling Trees;
> The trembling Trees, in ev'ry Plain and Wood,
> Her Fate remurmur to the silver Flood;
> The silver Flood, so lately calm, appears
> Swell'd with new Passion, and o'erflows with Tears.
> (*Winter*, 61–66)

Such a use of overlapping repetition is too heavy and
artificial for modern ears, as it was for Pope's, and he
never again used this figure in such a stiffly decorative
and literal manner. To see how much Pope learned in a
short time one can compare the opening eighteen lines
of the *Essay on Criticism*, where one couplet takes up
the terms of the preceding one and develops them in a
more fluid and subtle manner than does the previous
mincing rhetoric.

An example of the *epizeuxis* or *adjunctio*, in which the
synonym of a word is repeated in place of the word itself
in a slightly different sense, is this couplet which we have
already noted as defining the theme of *Summer:*

> This harmless Grove no lurking Viper hides,
> But in my Breast the Serpent Love abides.
> (Summer, 67–68)

This figure has great possibilities, but Pope sometimes
becomes too florid with it. He can write a fine couplet
describing the beauty of winter in terms of the deflow-
ered spring and summer,

> Behold the *Groves* that shine with silver Frost,
> Their Beauty wither'd and their Verdure lost,
> (Winter, 9–10)

and then fail a few lines later:

> Now hung with Pearls the dropping Trees appear,
> Their faded Honours scatter'd on her Bier.
> See, where on Earth the flowr'y Glories lye,
> With her they flourish'd, and with her they dye.
> (Winter, 31–34)

The abstractions of the first couplet, "Beauty wither'd" and "Verdure lost," are set in the context of the couplet; and there is a cause–effect relation between the shining silver frost and the fallen leaves. The generalizing balance of the second line is a pleasant contrast with the undivided first line. In the second passage, except for the good first line, the simple abstractions have become slightly puffed, epic-heroic periphrasis, "faded Honours" and "flow'ry Glories," which suggests a definite limit to how many synonyms Pope's shepherds can use for fallen leaves.

These by no means exhaust the number of figures in the poems, but we need no longer be detained by others, since Pope was working with two, chiasmus and zeugma, that he used with great satiric skill later on. Indeed, the techniques of parallelism we have seen thus far subsume chiasmus and zeugma, since these two figures are forms of balance and parallelism. On the whole Pope's use of chiasmus is sharp and effective, as in the final couplet of *Summer*,

> On me Love's fiercer Flames for ever prey,
> By Night he scorches, as he burns by Day,

but not always:

> Blest Swains, Whose Nymphs in ev'ry Grace excell;
> Blest Nymphs, Whose Swains those Graces sing so well!
> (*Spring*, 95–96)

Obviously the length and rigidity of this form makes it stilted and artificial, and Pope abandoned it.

At present a structure is called a chiasmus in which the second line repeats the structure of the first line with some degree of reversal of the main terms, or in which the second half of a line repeats the structure of the first half. The true classical chiasmus, however, calls for the strict reversal of the order of the main terms as in the second line of this example:

> Let other Swains attend the Rural Care,
> Feed fairer Flocks, or richer Fleeces share,
> (*Summer*, 35–36)

where the chiastic order of the verb "feed" and "share" throws a pun upon "share," to shear. Later Pope was to find this figure useful in making satirical thrusts, as this smash of the would-be wit in the fourth book of the *Dunciad*:

> Whate'er of mungril no one class admits,
> A wit with dunces, and a dunce with wits.
> (89–90)

The "mongrel" is made to seem doubly disgraceful when split by the chiasmus. Quickly and neatly he is twice a dunce because of the shifting perspective of the two terms as each changes its satiric focus from singular to plural and then from plural to singular.

Zeugma, the use of a yoking or controlling word that throws two or more terms into parallelism, served Pope more constantly in succeeding works than chiasmus. Technically zeugma is the grammatical linking of two words that cannot literally be used in the same sense; and the zeugma word is usually an adjective or adverb, as in "with sorrowful heads and hearts," or "with faint hearts and feet." At present zeugma is understood to include both this technical sense and the more common use of a single verb to throw two words into a witty or incongruous relation.[9]

Pope more often than not uses the verb as the yoking word in various positions. The following are typical of the *Pastorals:*

In Spring the Fields, in Autumn Hills I love. (*Spring,* 77)

Nor Plains at Morn, nor Groves at Noon delight.
(*Spring,* 80)

Now Leaves the Trees, and Flow'rs adorn the Ground.[10]
(*Spring,* 43)

If an incongruous equivalent is substituted in place of one of these agreeing nouns, the satiric possibilities of zeugma are obvious; and one gets the famous instance from the *Rape of the Lock:* "Or stain her Honour, or her new Brocade." (*Canto II,* 107).

Except for chiasmus and zeugma, Pope's first use of the figures is an experiment and little more. For the most part they are stilted and mechanical, especially the *reduplicato,* and sometimes the chiasmus. Too often the reader's attention is captured by the figures rather than the sense, and by the tricky parallelism of words rather than the integral balance and parallelism of real ideas and emotions. After the *Pastorals* Pope dropped most of the longer and more artificial figures and made chiasmus and zeugma a technique of creation rather than display.

In addition to developing techniques of balance and parallelism and experimenting with the figures of rhetoric, Pope was cleaning up the versification of the couplet, correcting technically the looser couplets of the seventeenth century poets. As Geoffrey Tillotson has remarked, "there was much still to do on the couplet when Pope began to write."[11] Tillotson has said that in spite of

Dryden's artistry with the couplet he did not advance it
beyond Waller except in onomatopoetic versification.[12]
In some ways Dryden "helped the measure to revert to a
freer form resembling, in rough and ready convenience,
the couplets of the Elizabethans."[13]

Everyone knows that Pope endeavored to follow William Walsh's advice in striving to be a "correct" poet.
We do not need here to seek a definition of what Pope
meant by this term, but merely to note that for Pope it
meant in a general way exactness, accuracy, and more
comprehensively, flawlessness of design and expression.
It is not a simple term, but means something a little
different in each kind of Pope's poetry. Nevertheless, in
versification it meant a retrenching, regularizing, or
tightening up after the freer couplet structure of Dryden.
At the beginning of his career, Pope expressed himself
about correct versification in letters to Walsh and to
Cromwell. It is clear that he had his predecessors in
mind; for most of the practices he wished to avoid are
precisely those of which Denham, Waller, and Dryden
were guilty. Pope emphasized the following principles:

1. Hiatus was to be avoided as often as possible, unless
   avoiding it made the sound too rough or awkward.
   (Pope's example prefers the hiatus in this line,
   "But the Old have Interest ever in their View,"
   rather than "th' Old" which Pope considered
   clumsy and stiff.)
2. All expletives were to be avoided such as "do" before plural verbs, and the too frequent use of "did"
   and "does" to change the termination of a line or
   rhyme.
3. Since monosyllables were to Pope "stiff, languish-

ing and hard," they had to be managed artfully and not used too frequently.

4. Rhymes should not be repeated within four or six lines of each other because they would tire the ear.
5. Alexandrines were to be used very sparingly and only when necessary for "majesty" or added sense.
6. The caesura should be placed on the fourth, fifth, or sixth syllables and the same caesura should not be continued for more than three consecutive lines.
7. The sound should fit the sense of what is treated. In describing a gliding stream, "the numbers should run easy and flowing," and "in describing a rough Torrent or Deluge," they should be "sonorous and swelling."[14]

If the successful application of the first six principles was all that Pope had accomplished technically in the couplet form, his style would be far less interesting. The profounder and problematic seventh principle, although Pope states it too simply and generally, is not a technical and mechanical one in the sense that the others are and need not detain us here since we will meet it again under many guises. Fortunately Pope consistently and successfully violates most of his principles except the second, fifth, and sixth, and his violations prove his rules too strict.[15] What is frustrating, however, about this list of prescriptions, and indeed about most of Pope's remarks on the couplet, is that he never wrote of such crucial things as rhyme, balance, antithesis, zeugma, or chiasmus.[16] He remarked on rhyme only that he doubted whether English poetry could function without the "support" of rhyme unless poetry were "stiffened with such strange words as are likely to destroy our language itself."[17] Since the perfection of form he wrought in the couplet (even the *Pastorals*) is more basic and comprehensive than the correction of mere faults of versification, his conception of the faults of his predecessors, after whom he was correcting, must have taken in more than the violations of such rules as those listed in his letters to Walsh and Cromwell. The task, therefore, of refining and tightening the structure of the couplet beyond anything that Denham, Waller, and Dryden had accomplished was for Pope either a necessary labor too obvious for comment, or the various techniques of parallelism were so familiar to him from his early years and so much a part of his stylistic heritage that he was largely unconscious of honing parallelism into a tauter, sharper instrument.

Because of Pope's intense interest in correct versification and his concern to avoid the more noticeable and monotonous practices of his predecessors, one would expect him in his first work to eschew expletives, Alexandrines, and triplets; and compared with later works the *Pastorals* employ very few monosyllabic lines. He believed at the beginning of his career in rigid placing of the caesura and achieved it in the *Pastorals*; he was less successful in avoiding monotonous rhymes such as "sing–spring." But what one does not expect in so young a poet toiling in Dryden's shadow is the escape from the structure of Dryden's couplets and the flowing designs of his great passages. Pope was clinically successful in eluding Dryden's run-on, open constructions, his more weaving syntax, his "mighty line"; and while creating some couplet structures of his own, he avoided Dryden's faults, as well as some of his virtues. It was not until later that Pope, the seasoned master, would achieve in his distinctive way the majesty and energy of his great predecessor.

But more important than suppressing the influence of Dryden's more luxuriant couplet style, a feat of skill and discipline, Pope demonstrated his stylistic mastery by making his couplet reflect the design of his four poems. In accordance with his four seasons, he seldom lets his couplets stagnate or grow monotonous; the dominant parallelism is varied enough with other structures to suggest differences of theme and the "particular beauty in every Eclogue." The smooth, linear compound sentence structures of the couplet norm help to suggest the quiet beauty of the scenes and the harmonious relations of the shepherds to their pastoral world. The more pointed forms of antithesis add a quality of harshness and brittleness to the poems, creating a degree of stylistic variety and tension that suggests the element of conflict between man and woman and between man and nature. Mainly Pope proved himself a master of couplet structure in two complementary ways: he learned how to write neat parallel lines superior in their concision and directness to the couplets of his predecessors, and how to diversify and sharpen this simple compounding parallelism with balanced antithesis, chiasmus, and zeugma. Pope had tested his couplet instrument; and like his great contemporary Johann Sebastian Bach, who "tested" the clavichord, Pope found that his couplet, fine as it was, needed a "tempered tuning" and deeper music.

NOTES

1. A *Discourse on Pastoral Poetry, Twick. Ed.,* I, eds. E. Audra and Aubrey Williams (1961), 24–25.

2. *Ibid.,* p. 25.

3. Introduction to A *Discourse on Pastoral Poetry, ibid.,* p. 15.

4. A *Discourse on Pastoral Poetry, ibid.,* pp. 27–28.

5. Audra and Williams point out that Spenser's general plan in the *Shepherds Calendar,* though modified by Pope, contributes to the structure of the poem as a whole, and that "the theme of time, and of the changes wrought by time is central to the scheme of these poems [the *Pastorals*]." Introduction to *Pastorals, op. cit.,* pp. 49–50.

6. "Eighteenth-Century Poetic Diction," *Eighteenth Century English Literature, Modern Essays in Criticism,* ed. James L. Clifford (New York: Oxford University Press, 1959), pp. 219–20.

7. Audra and Williams, *op. cit.,* pp. 49–50.

8. *Alexander Pope: The Poetry of Allusion* (Oxford: Oxford University Press, 1959), p. 23.

9. Wimsatt's discussion of Pope's use of zeugma in "Rhetoric and Poems," *The Verbal Icon,* is most helpful and interesting.

10. I borrow the second and third examples from Tillotson, *On the Poetry of Pope,* p. 128.

11. *Ibid.,* p. 105.

12. *Ibid.,* p. 112.

13. *Ibid.,* p. 105.

14. *The Correspondence of Alexander Pope,* ed. George Sherburn (Oxford and New York, Oxford University Press, 1956), Vol. I, "Pope to Walsh" (Oct. 22, 1706), 22–25; "Pope to Cromwell," (Nov. 25, 1710), pp. 106–07.

15. Jacob H. Adler, "Pope and the Rules of Prosody," *Publications of the Modern Language Association,* LXXVI (1961), 218–26. Adler has shown conclusively that Pope's letters on prosody did not reflect his own practice and that he followed broad general principles rather than strict narrow rules. See also Adler's later study, *The Reach of Art: A Study in the Prosody of Pope* (Gainesville: University of Florida Press, 1964).

16. Pope's treatment of versification is much more sophisticated in *An Essay on Criticism* than in the letters to Walsh and Cromwell, but he still refuses to mention some of his most interesting and distinctive practices of couplet structure.

17. Joseph Spence, *Anecdotes, Observations, and Characters of Books and Men,* 2nd ed. (London: John Russell Smith, 1858), p. 212.

3

An *Essay* on *Criticism* 1711

In 1711, two years after the *Pastorals*, came the *Essay on Criticism*, a work astonishing in its verve and brilliance when we remember that Pope was only twenty-three and had certainly written much of the *Essay* some two years earlier.[1] The contrast between the two works is considerable. The *Pastorals* are restricted in subject and style; the *Essay on Criticism* is more varied and realistic because it treats the particulars of literary history and practice. The rather brittle style of the first poems gave way two years later to a style more relaxed and conversational, which employed fewer tropes and figures and more variations of couplet structure in less constricted sentence forms. The style of the *Pastorals* is masterful—and labored; that of the *Essay* is equally masterful, less labored, and shows a growing adeptness in handling various tones and modes of discourse. Significantly, the style of the *Essay* is Pope's way of looking at literature, and as we shall see, adds indispensable richness and color to the argumentative and persuasive framework of the poem.

The wit of the *Essay on Criticism* has been deceptive; for Pope's famous aphorisms and gems of "proverbial" wisdom are frequently interpreted out of their contexts.

The unwary reader is misled by the urbane surface of the poem and is tempted to an easy reading which the skill of Pope's couplets seems to invite. To such a reader the poem is likely to appear a tame "neoclassic" compromise, wittily urged, in which Pope takes an impregnably safe stance. He looks to the ancients for guidance and praises modern writers too. He pays homage to the rules and turns the other way to salute genius breaking the rules; and he produces a series of entertaining statements about wit that reduces it to a variety of ornament and decoration in keeping with the late seventeenth-century decline of rhetoric as a serious intellectual discipline and wit as a creative faculty. Looked at superficially, the *Essay* says everything, or nothing, because Pope's positions seem contradictory. But if Pope is sometimes equivocal, his Janus stance is firmly based, one can say, upon his awareness of the complex nature of literature as a viable human "product." Obviously by today's standards the *Essay* gives a limited treatment of literary theory and critical principles. Yet Pope's immersion in the problems raised in the poem is always sprightly and humane, and furthermore the incisiveness of his antithetic treatment of writing and judging, in all its "Euclidean" manifestations,[2] makes the *Essay on Criticism* a unique poem of its kind.

The ideal toward which everything in the *Essay* points is one of wholeness and corporateness since the critic, and the poet too, must be whole in Pope's classical and humanist sense in order to meet on the common ground of Nature and therefore to write and criticize significantly.[3] To emphasize the ideal of wholeness, Pope first throws into relief the oppositions in the literary disputes of his times, polarizing such important pairs of terms as poet–critic, wit–judgment, whole–part, inspiration–rules, ancient–modern. His method of handling these oppositions creates the couplet norm of the poem—a closed couplet with a balanced antithesis that appears about half the time in sharply balanced and discrete hemistichs and about half the time in a more oblique syntax. Within his tightly drawn parallels, Pope sets the antithetic relations which fragment his ideal of Nature; but these antithetic couplets usually point to some larger meaning or reality than that of either part of the antithesis. For this reason the *Essay on Criticism* is more than a flashy exposition of supposed neoclassic principles which turn upon the clever antithesis of a restricted group of literary concepts. One must notice not only Pope's orchestration of such terms as wit, judgment, and rules, but the suggestive power of his complex parallelism. The whole tenor of Pope's antithetic parallelism is to a "reconciliation of opposites" within the ideal principle of Nature.

Pope's couplet style, as in the later *Essay on Man*, ranges from the informal and conversational, through a middle style of exposition, to a grand public manner. Throughout the poem he shifts from one manner to another in accordance with his persuasive purposes; but no matter what his tone or manner, balanced antithesis, except in the closing lines of the poem, is the norm from which he sometimes departs and to which he always returns. Since the argumentative structure of the *Essay* is so well known, a lengthy or systematic and chronological examination of the *Essay's* norm couplets would be rather useless and tedious. My method in this chapter,

therefore, will be to look at the main characteristics of
some of Pope's norm couplets, and then at the main
variation.

To open the poem, Pope weaves two main threads of
the *Essay*, "writing [ill]" and "judging ill," into a brilliant symbiotic pattern of opposition:

> 'Tis hard to say, if greater Want of Skill
> 2 Appear in *Writing* or in *Judging* ill;
> But, of the two, less dang'rous is th' Offence,
> 4 To tire our *Patience*, than mis-lead our Sense:
> Some few in *that*, but Numbers err in *this*,
> 6 Ten Censure wrong for one who Writes amiss;
> A *Fool* might once *himself* alone expose,
> 8 Now *One* in *Verse* makes many more in *Prose*.
>
> (1–8)

In these lines Pope employs a general chiastic structure,
not a rigid or symmetrical one. After "*Writing* [ill]" and
Judging ill" appear in the second line, the pair undergoes
a process of analysis or shifting perspective through the
remainder of the passage. Except for the first, third, and
seventh, each line contains a balance, one-half about
writing ill and the other half about judging ill; and each
of these terms is "translated" in each couplet, its synonym occurring as half of the parallel. Through a series
of shifting, parallel synonyms, "Writing [ill]" becomes
at the end of the paragraph " One [fool] in *Verse*"; and
"*Judging* ill" becomes "many more [fools] in *Prose*."
With each occurrence, each term means something
slightly different; and the primary terms have been transferred by a series of steps from their somewhat neutral
existence in the second line to a pernicious public effect
in the sixth. "Want of Skill," the initial subject of the
first line, has been split into its twin components (writ-

ing and judging), refracted through the parallels; and,
since its owners make it publicly known, emerges in the
last line as "fools." Ironically the clashing antithesis between critic and poet is reconciled; for writing ill and
judging ill finally produce an inevitable resolution—
fools.

The structures of the second paragraph are similar,
and Pope leads directly into his examination of the "partiality" of critics:

> 'Tis with our *Judgments* as our *Watches*, none
> 2 Go just *alike*, yet each believes his own.
>   In *Poets* as true *Genius* is but rare,
> 4 True *Taste* as seldom is the *Critick's* Share;
>   Both must alike from Heav'n derive their Light,
> 6 These *born* to Judge, as well as those to Write.
>   Let such teach others who themselves excell,
> 8 And *censure freely* who have *written well.*
>   *Authors* are partial to their *Wit*, 'tis true,
> 10 But are not *Criticks* to their *Judgment* too?
>   (9–18)

Pope suggests with the off-rhyme "none," which carries
the run-on imbalance of the halves of the second line,
that there is a kind of odd imbalance in men's judg-
ments. In the second couplet, "Poets–Criticks" and
"Taste–Genius" are parallel in a chiasmus; and since
both poets and critics lack taste and genius, the pointed
rhyme suggests a "rare share" of either. In the third
couplet "Light," a larger consideration in Pope's scheme
than the oppositions within the couplet dominates the
balance that follows. The ambiguous penultimate couplet seems to contradict the preceding one, but it is
"excelling well" that stands out, not teaching and censur-
ing; and in the last couplet, "partial," although in an

unemphatic position, is emphasized because it is the
zeugma word which yokes authors and critics into parallelism. To partiality in wit and judgment, the interlock-
ing balances have been moving from the start. The
design of this two-paragraph opening suggests a complicated formal dance: as one couplet follows another, the
two terms of each balance give way to new equivalents
and new balances that change the reader's angle of vision
with each succeeding balance.

The balances of the opening prefigure the couplet
style of the whole poem. The sharp counterpointing of
ideas is spread out and strategically diffused; and the
couplet norm employs double-edged thrusts which create
not only the exposition of the poem, but humorous paradox, and vehement eloquence.

The additional examples of the couplet norm given
below illustrate Pope's literary and critical viewpoint,
which is neoclassical in the best senses of this term. But
this perspicacious viewpoint is frequently varied by
Pope's bursts of enthusiasm and shafts of mischief. In
addition, he sometimes revels in paradox; it is no wonder
he confused a grimly serious reader like John Dennis. In
sampling Pope's lines, let us take first an acidulous statement about the competitive spirit of incompetent writers:

> Each burns alike, who can, or cannot write,
> Or with a *Rival's*, or an *Eunuch's* spite.   (30–31)

The second line translates and sharpens the first and
deflates "Each" with a humiliating comparison that
works two ways. By shifting the comparison from performance in writing to performance in love, the spite of

the impotent writer becomes doubly shameful. *"Rival's* [spite]" and *"Eunuch's* spite" are different things to begin with, and are made antithetical in an additional sense because they are governed respectively by "can" and "cannot." Neither should have spite, and they should not have it for different reasons. The antithesis, however, is thrown into another perspective by the yoking verb "burns" which emphasizes the contrasts between the two main nouns. Both the rival and the eunuch are despicable for different reasons; and both "burn" for the wrong reasons, but are condemned for the right reason—"spite." No reader, of course, goes through such a "Euphuistic" and tiresome process of analysis as this when he reads the poem, but these multiple cross-references lie just under the surface of Pope's cutting parallels.

The fumblers, those who can write neither poetry nor criticism, draw upon themselves a comparison that not only emphasizes the hollowness of would-be literary people's pretensions, but goes further to imply a sterility as insulting as possible:

> Some neither can for *Wits* nor *Criticks* pass,
> As heavy Mules are neither *Horse* nor *Ass.*
>
> (38–39)

The two terms in the first line are paralleled and given damaging equivalents by the third term "Mules." *"Horse"* and *"Ass"* recoil upon "Mules"—part horse, part ass. The subjects of the couplet can pass for neither since like a mule they are sterile hybrids, beings at odds with ordinary nature. By implication Pope's equation plays with nature: the physical nature of the mule is a kind of deviation from the norm just as the insistent

incompetence of literary pretenders is a deviation from
Pope's Nature as the "source," "end," and "test" of art.

These two couplets illustrate Pope's skill with antithetic couplets that pivot upon constructions controlled
by "each," "neither–nor," "either–or," "some–few," and
so on. One of the alternatives controls a line or half line,
and its counterpart directs the completion. In the preceding "rival and eunuch" couplet, "Each" sets off a
chain reaction; and by the end of the couplet "Each" has
been split into four parts by the direction of "can,"
"cannot," and "or." In the second couplet, "Ass receives
the same syntactic emphasis as "Horse," but the conno-
tation pulls the denotation out of place: a heavy mule is
no more ass than horse; but in spite of the impartial
genetic comparison in the first line, the writers are, from
a rhetorical standpoint, asses.

Frequently antithesis is not made by parallel terms
that pivot upon alternating words as above, but it works
ambiguously in a muted syntax as in the following example where the chiastic structure of "profuse–want" and
"Wit–it" varies the clashing balances of many norm
couplets:

> Some, to whom Heav'n in Wit has been profuse,
> Want as much more, to turn it to its use.   (80–81)

The structure helps the realization of the couplet's
meaning. The apparently neutral syntax and concealed
chiasmus achieve Pope's strategy of springing the paradox that annihilates the artificial distinction between wit
as the creative faculty and judgment as the retrenching,
analytical faculty. E. N. Hooker has noted that the paradox of these lines lends itself to ridicule, but that with

his marvelous gift of lucidity to aid him, Pope chose to leave the couplet as it is because even against the criticism of Dennis, it seemed the best way of expressing something that was very difficult.[4] Pope did not intend to slip into the Lockean pitfall of separating wit and judgment; and as Audra and Williams point out in the Twickenham Edition of the poem, against the prevailing temper of the times, the couplet suggests a reconstitution of wit and judgment into a common creative faculty.[5]

Another couplet on wit is easily the most famous, or the most notorious, in the *Essay:*

> *True Wit* is *Nature* to Advantage drest,
> What oft was *Thought,* but ne'er so well *Exprest.*
>
> (297–98)

Dr. Johnson charged of this couplet that Pope depresses wit below its true dignity, and then went on to give a definition of wit which embraces the implications about the term that Pope had strewn throughout the *Essay.*[6] Unfortunately, many readers have followed Johnson's lead, feeling that Pope meant by *True Wit* the ornamentation of a proverbial commonplace. E. N. Hooker's evaluation of Pope's position deserves to be quoted at this point, for it explains clearly what Pope's famous couplet summarizes:

> To define wit, therefore, as 'What oft was thought, but ne'er so well expressed,' does not say or imply that wit is a stale or commonplace thought nicely tricked out. The definition rather supposes that the writer, starting with a common and universal experience, sees it in a new light; and his sensitive spirit, endowing it with life and fresh meaning, provides it with form, image, language, and harmony appropriate to it. It presupposes the liveliness

and insight of the creative mind; and it demands propriety, the perfect agreement of words, thoughts (as
reshaped by the artist), and subject. The result is nature,
and it is wit.[7]

Like many other aphoristic couplets in Pope's works, the
one on *"True Wit"* is ambiguous when taken alone, and
one can argue that it is, in fact, a pejorative statement
about wit by seventeenth- and twentieth-century standards. But when one examines it in the context of Pope's
general discussion of Nature (ll. 68–79, 141–160,
233–252), and against the lines immediately preceding
the couplet itself,

> Poets like Painters, thus, unskill'd to trace
> The *naked Nature* and the *living Grace*,
> With *Gold* and *Jewels* cover ev'ry Part,
> And hide with *Ornaments* their *Want of Art*,
> (293–96)

it is clear that Hooker's evaluation is sound. While
Pope's conception of wit is different from that of Donne
or T. S. Eliot, it is nevertheless a more complex conception than that of Hobbes or Locke, whose discussions of
wit Pope was certainly familiar with.[8] Such is the calcu-
lated casualness of the *Essay* that sometimes Pope will
boldly spring a paradox as in the couplet on wit managing wit, or he will make a statement such as the one on
"True Wit," depending on the alertness of the reader to
understand its relation to other passages. The couplet on
"True Wit" works a simpler syntax than some, but it has
Pope's characteristic balance. Actually the couplet has a
chiastic order. The parallels of the second line rebound
simultaneously upon the separate terms *"Wit"* and

"*Nature*" in chiastic order, and upon the whole first line because of the equivalence of "*True Wit*" and "*Nature*." The equivalence of the parallels suggests an algebraic equation, yet, as Pope shows throughout his poem, the content of this equation is always changing. Thus Pope drives home in an almost "representational" balance and parallelism the sense of unity that underlies the antithesis of the poem.

Sometimes antithesis that reflects unity and synthesis is insidiously plain, as in this couplet which follows and illuminates the one on wit managing wit:

> For *Wit* and *Judgment* often are at Strife,
> Tho' meant each other's Aid, like *Man* and *Wife*.
> (82–83)

This type of disarming, homely comparison is found regularly if not frequently all through the poem. Pope suddenly drops from abstract discussion and urbane literary talk to the human confrontation of man and wife. Wit and judgment are integral parts of creative imagination just as man and wife are integral, not disparate, parts of love and marriage. Pope does not mean to be trivial, to reduce a complexity to a cliché, but to suggest that his conception of Nature and of genius unifies wit and judgment just as marriage unifies man and woman.

The analogy between husband–wife and wit–judgment is repeated with a variation in a couplet that asserts an inversion of values brought about by wits who at last became critics because they could not become poets:

> But following Wits from that Intention stray'd;
> Who cou'd not win the Mistress, woo'd the Maid.
> (104–05)

To follow the rhyme, the incompetent wit "strayed to
the maid," an instance of Pope's rhyme where the first
rhyme, though end-stopped, carries over the action onto
the second rhyme word. This is one of Pope's favorite
structures where the two halves of the balance slice apart
the general and rather neutral statement of the first line
into witty and unusual particulars, which, in this example, create a laxness in the victims that is tinged with
humorous disgrace. In this couplet,

> Those oft are *Stratagems* which *Errors* seem,
> Nor is it *Homer Nods,* but *We* that *Dream,*
>   (179–80)

the second line drops from the general to concrete application; and the parallels, while drawn up sharply, tele-
scope into each other. When one considers the equivalence of nouns and verbs, the paradoxes soon multiply
and the parallels suggest a room of mirrors. The torqued
equivalents, however, are appropriate where the degree
of an author's *supposed* faults is equal to the same degree
of a reader's ignorance. It is a game of the multiplica-
tion of negatives.

Wit has different aspects in the *Essay,* each possessing
or creating a different kind of problem. In the next
example Pope turns with a mixture of sarcasm and despair to note in a flippant metaphor wit's different requirements in writer and reader:

> What is this Wit which must our Cares employ?
> The *Owner's Wife,* that *other Men* enjoy.
>   (500–01)

The cross-reference of active and passive works effectively. Both the rhyming verbs are active, but in the

second line the subordinate clause makes the owner's wife passive rather than active. Like a wife, wit commands or employs the writer's cares; but another man (the reader who is under no obligation to decipher the writer's meaning) can take her and enjoy her without cares, just as the poet labors on a work for a year so the reader can "ravish" it in an hour. So wit is the poet's wife, but the reader's mistress! But Pope's mischievous couplet implies that she is still a woman, still Nature; and critic and poet share and experience her, but in appropriately different ways.

These norm couplets that we have sampled polarize the parts of ideas that for Pope and his times were basic conceptions in criticism. They suddenly gather up and crystallize oppositions; but there is usually a cross-reference, a rebounding chiasmus of some sort in the couplet showing that Pope recognized the overlapping or telescoping relations of the antithetic concepts. Clearly he wished to express these relations in parallels whose antithetic terms are related to one another by complex cross-references in order to make the sharp, neat, prose-like syntax of the couplets emerge finally with the sense of paradox and ambiguity inherent in the creative process of both critic and poet, reader and writer.

If the *Essay on Criticism* employed a majority of couplets whose parallels are as complex and geometric as those of the norm couplets, the poem would be an overpowering piece of virtuosity from which the reader would recoil, irritated and amazed. But the norm couplets are strategically placed, and the poem is varied with passages whose lines are neutral of antithetic balance. The *Essay*, we should not forget, is a piece of graceful persuasion, and Pope begins to show ease and facility with elliptical constructions, with subordination, and with series of open couplets which contrast the couplet norm. For instance, two passages, each of which contains one of the previous norm couplets, illustrate Pope's growing mastery of modulation:

> Some have at first for *Wits*, then *Poets* past,
> 2 Turn'd *Criticks* next, and prov'd plain *Fools* at last;
> Some neither can for *Wits* nor *Criticks* pass,
> 4 As heavy Mules are neither *Horse* nor *Ass*.
> Those half-learn'd Witlings, num'rous in our Isle,
> 6 As half-form'd Insects on the Banks of *Nile*;
> Unfinish'd Things, one knows not what to call,
> 8 Their Generation's so *equivocal*:
> To tell 'em wou'd a *hundred Tongues* require,
> 10 Or *one vain Wit*'s, that might a hundred tire.
>
> (36–45)

In the third and fourth couplets Pope turns suddenly from his closed parallels, drops to a conversational tone, and holds up the completion of the thought until the final couplet falls into place almost as a careless afterthought.

In passages of open couplets, Pope employs fewer balances and his lines grow more sustained and eloquent than in the closed couplets. This is a new development, and Pope unleashes a vehemence lacking in the *Pastorals*. A passage on the relation of the writer to his public, an aspect of wit in its social context, will illustrate this point:

> What is this *Wit* which must our Cares employ?
> 2 The *Owner's Wife*, that *other Men* enjoy,
> Then most our *Trouble* still when most *admir'd*,
> 4 And still the more we *give*, the more *requir'd*;
> Whose Fame with *Pains* we guard, but lose with *Ease*,

6 Sure *some* to *vex*, but never *all* to *please;*
  'Tis what the *Vicious fear,* the *Virtuous shun;*
8 By *Fools* 'tis *hated,* and by *Knaves undone!*

(500–07)

After the first couplet suggests that the owner is in trou-
ble, the hovering antithesis of the next two couplets
works in an unusual manner. The parallels employ a sort
of treadmill action; and the statement of each half line is
obliterated by its following parallel, as in the fourth line
where the second "more" cancels the first while increasing the demand upon the first "more." Then in the last
couplet this curious, slipping motion which gets nowhere
changes to a series of swift parallels. The inversion in
both halves of the last line suddenly emphasizes the two
pairs of nouns and verbs, and *"hated"* and *"undone"*
achieve a stinging climax. As the passage unfolds its
meaning, the couplets employ successively complicated
paradox, antithesis, and negation; but the movement,
expressive of Pope's frustration and disdain, is swift, sure,
and conclusive.

Pope, of course, breaks from his balanced parallels,
although not as freely as he was to do later. The famous
passage on the breaking of the rules is the best example
of the different design that occurs now and then in the
poem and is noticeable for the absence of the norm
couplets:

Some Beauties yet, no Precepts can declare,
2 For there's a *Happiness* as well as *Care.*
  Musick resembles *Poetry,* in each ⎫
4 Are *nameless Graces* which no Methods teach, ⎬
  And which a *Master-Hand* alone can reach. ⎭

 6 If, where the *Rules* not far enough extend,
   (Since Rules were made but to promote their End)
 8 Some Lucky LICENCE answers to the full
   Th' Intent propos'd, *that Licence* is a *Rule.*
10 Thus *Pegasus,* a nearer way to take,
   May boldly deviate from the common Track.
12 Great Wits sometimes may *gloriously offend,*
   And *rise* to *Faults* true Criticks *dare not mend:*
14 From *vulgar Bounds* with *brave Disorder part,*
   And *snatch a Grace* beyond the Reach of Art,
16 Which, without passing thro' the *Judgment,* gains
   The *Heart,* and all its End *at once* attains.   (141–57)

There are no balances in the first half of this passage.
The first line of the triplet is imbalanced and run-on, as
is the eighth line. At the tenth line the passage gathers
itself for its "Pegasian" flight; and the last three couplets
(12–17) are one swift unit in which great wits perform
appropriate actions: *"offend," "rise," "part,"* and
"snatch." "Grace" is the object of the verbs, and when
this object is seized, it then becomes the subject of another set of verbs and "gains The *Heart*" in a run-on line,
achieving its end "all at once," literally. *"Heart,"* a good
example of internal rhyme, welds the last two couplets in
an additional sense. It is the "part" to be gained by a
certain stroke of "art"; so "art–part–heart" is a loose,
rhyming paradigm of the meaning of the couplets. The
axiomatic and fine proselike couplets about rules give
way to a swift, open passage whose movement suggests
its meaning.

   In a similar passage, also a famous one, Pope holds up
to the critic the light of Nature:

   First follow NATURE, and your Judgment frame
   By her just Standard, which is still the same:
   Unerring Nature, still divinely bright,

One *clear, unchang'd,* and *Universal* Light,
Life, Force, and Beauty, must to all impart,
At once the *Source,* and *End,* and *Test* of Art.
Art from that Fund each *just Supply* provides,
Works *without Show,* and *without Pomp* presides:
In some fair Body thus th' informing Soul
With Spirits feeds, with Vigour fills the whole,
Each Motion guides, and ev'ry Nerve sustains;
It self unseen, but in th' *Effects* remains.   (68–79)

The flowing, neutral parallelism of this passage is a good example of Pope's expansion of his sentence beyond the closed couplet, and of his recognition since the *Pastorals* that every couplet does not need a separate predication with explicit grammar. Both passages emphasize the unity and wholeness toward which Pope pulls his antithesis, for at the moment of insight or inspiration genius looks into the heart of Nature, "One *clear, unchang'd,* and *Universal Light.*" Balanced antithesis with its analytical functions is, at the moment, transcended.

Pope departs from his thematically dominant balance only a few times: in the two key passages we have just examined; in the famous passage on versification with its examples of representative meter on sound and sense (337–73); in the paean to the ancients closing Part I (181–200); and in the final fifty lines of the poem where he briefly sketches in flowing parallels the revival of literature and art in the Italian Renaissance (697–704); praises Roscommon (719–28); and goes on to end the poem by paying homage to Walsh, who was free of the divisive flaws and "partialities" which form so much of the subject of the Essay. The balanced antithesis of the final lines lacks the sharpness and paradox of the norm couplets which would be, at this point, inappropriate to the forward rush and vehemence of the language of praise; and in the closing lines Pope has ostensibly achieved his rhetorical purpose.

The structure or "plot" of the *Essay* suggests the decline of wit—creative genius in either poetry or criticism —from the harmony of opposing forces achieved by the ancients, which is a form of Nature, into separate embodiments of wit and judgment, poet and critic. Then it goes on to show a further shattering of this harmony into aesthetic and moral faults such as judging by parts rather than wholes, and judging the author or a semblance of the work rather than the work itself. But Pope, as we have seen, insists throughout upon integration of wit and judgment into a common faculty, and, as a literary and critical ideal, upon the aesthetic and moral wholeness characteristic of the great ancients. Pope's dominant mode of balanced antithesis subtly supports his theme of unity and wholeness. His parallels, which play with antithetic concepts of genius and art, such as wit–judgment, and poet–critic, are opposed in couplet form, making the opposition sharp and clear. But these oppositions are always related and attracted to each other (like man and wife), and Pope makes the effort to reconcile them by the use of couplets turning upon ambiguous antitheses which suggest that no matter what their oppositions seem to be, wit and judgment, poet and critic, are manifestations of the same creative power. The critic or poet who is a good man and a wise one, in Pope's classical and humanist sense, will hold and contain in balance the antithesis of the poem, just as the bow gains its essence from the tension of its string. If this resulting wise man seems a little austere, many of Pope's couplets make it clear that he should practice his art with charm, with good humor, and even with a touch of "wit." Otherwise he is not quite complete as man or writer.

Compared with the balanced couplets of the *Essay on Criticism*, those of the *Pastorals* are simple and ingenuous. The witty deflations, alogical rhymes, and brilliant paradoxes of Pope's balances are appropriate to the less artificial *Essay* and to its wider range of subject and style. In the next poem, *Windsor-Forest*, Pope's artistry with parallelism yields surprisingly different results.

NOTES

1. Audra and Williams, Introduction to *An Essay on Criticism, Twick. Ed.* I, 197–202. My discussion of the *Essay on Criticism*, especially of its structure and design, is indebted to Audra and Williams.

2. I borrow this descriptive term from Geoffrey Tillotson's remarks on Pope's couplets in *Augustan Studies* (London: The Athlone Press, 1961), pp. 13–14.

3. See Maynard Mack's excellent discussion of this point: Introduction to *An Essay on Criticism*, "The Augustans," *English Masterpieces*, IV, 2nd ed. (Englewood Cliffs, New Jersey: Prentice-Hall, Inc., 1961), p. 21.

4. "Pope on Wit: The *Essay on Criticism*," *Eighteenth Century English Literature, Modern Essays in Criticism*, ed. James L. Clifford (New York: Oxford University Press, 1959), p. 52.

5. Audra and Williams, *op. cit.*, p. 218. Also Mack, *op. cit.*, p. 21.

6. In Johnson's brilliant and influential discussion of wit in "Abraham Cowley," *Lives of the English Poets*, I, Everyman, 10–12.

7. "Pope on Wit: The *Essay on Criticism*," p. 58.

8. See the excellent short discussion of Audra and Williams of the views of Hobbes and Locke on wit and fancy. *Op. cit.*, pp. 215–17.

4

❦

Windsor-Forest 1713

UNTIL RECENTLY most readers had been content to read *Windsor-Forest* as a descriptive–pastoral poem composed in two parts at different times. The first part, mostly descriptive and pastoral, described the forest itself as well as some important events in its history, and the second part rather blatantly celebrated the recent Peace of Utrecht. Such a reading is no longer tenable because any discussion or interpretation of the poem must base itself upon the work of Earl R. Wasserman and the editors of the *Twickenham Edition*. In a brilliant study, Wasserman has shown that *Windsor-Forest* is a complex, symbolic work, tightly coherent and unified.[1] According to Wasserman, the forest is the organizing and dynamic symbol of an ancient law of nature, the law of *concordia discors*, the active harmonizing of differences through strife. At every step and in its every aspect, the poem articulates this law as it operated in the forest; and like Sir John Dehham's Thames in *Cooper's Hill*, the forest itself is the ideal physical expression, in little, of this one law of nature.[2]

As the symbol of this law, the forest represents the operation of the law of *concordia discors* in two basic ways. First, the physical beauty of the forest with its variety of field, wood, hill, and stream is symbolic of the "harmonious confusion" of the world itself (ll. 11–16). Second the hunting scenes which take place in the forest in Queen Anne's reign represent "the dynamic principle in man, the energy without which he would stagnate, but which uncontrolled, produces chaos, just as William's [William the Conqueror] overzealous hunting impulses made a chaos out of the cosmic Windsor Forest."[3] These two basic instances of *concordia discors*—the natural "typographical" beauty of the forest itself, and the hunting which actually takes place in it—are contrasted with two main incidents: the violent history of the forest when its peace and liberty was shattered by the advent of the Norman kings, whose cruel and tyrannical rule finally gave way to a peaceful reign in which each man reaped the fruits of his labor and employed his arms on "birds and beasts alone"; and the myth of the nymph Lodona, who was metamorphosed by Pan when she strayed beyond the limits of the forest in search of prey. The nymph represents an unnatural excess of the human warring instinct—in particular, the excessive desire of the Whigs to continue the war against France when it was no longer necessary.

The value and meaning of the forest itself as the symbol of the law of *concordia discors* rests upon the idea of divine analogy, which is summarized by Audra and Williams in the *Twickenham Edition* of the poem:

> It is not simply by precedent alone, however, that Pope's fusion of the scenic, the moral, and the political is to be understood and justified. Pope was writing in a time when a vast system of analogical correspondences between God and man and nature was still in force.

This system "assumed that God, expressing Himself in all creation," had "made the physical, moral, and spiritual levels analogous to each other and to Himself." And because this was felt to be true, man, when he scanned the book of creation, could there discover analogues to his own moral and political experiences. Because all the links in the Chain of Being were similar, "joy and grief" could be "read in trees and plants," and "precepts of morality" could be "insinuated by reference to " 'those Faculties in the Souls of Brutes, which bear an Analogy to the Will and Passions. . . .' " This analogous relationship between all things enabled the imagination to discover, rather than merely to fabricate, similitudes between the natural world on the one hand, and the moral and political worlds on the other. In a poem like *Windsor-Forest* one cannot expect, nor does one often find, purely descriptive scenes of nature: the setting of the poem is always offering its analogue to human experience. It is not simply that the poem offers one a scene from nature and then injects into it a moral ethical prescription; the two elements are rather fused in the one act of perception, for the poet, in this instance is discovering meanings inherent in nature, not adding one thing to another.[4]

The poem is simultaneously general and particular; each of its scenes articulates in some manner the idea of analogical correspondence, and the controlling theme of *concordia discors*, which permeates the idea, moves simultaneously through the time and space of the poem: from a discordant past to a harmonious future; from the forest itself down the Thames to London; and finally in Father Thames' vision of the reign of Peace, from a just and peaceful England, to the whole wide world; that is, from the little to the great, from the particular to the ultimate generality.

One notices a general resemblance of the theme and

design of *Windsor-Forest* to that of the *Essay on Criticism*. In both poems Pope confronts basic and universal problems of relation that appear under a different semblance for every age and in every situation in which the separate and individual must be included in, and related to, a significant philosophic or religious pattern of some kind. The separateness and isolation that appear to be a condition of life, whether in the eighteenth or twentieth century, must be overcome or resolved. In the *Essay on Criticism* Pope reconciled oppositions of wit and judgment by a conception of literary creativity which fused separate powers of the mind into one force. The lines of discussion between wit and judgment that Pope already found drawn up were sharply demarked, however, and Pope cast his antithesis in balanced couplets and made the paradoxes explicit; so antithesis is often discursive and dialectic. In *Windsor-Forest* the sharp, formal rhetorical antithesis of literary terms and ideas is absent. Rather Pope builds antithesis by juxtaposing scenes whose antithetic relations are neither overt nor striking, or by introducing a discordant note into an apparently harmonious scene. Pope's aim is not the witty (but nonetheless realistic) discussion of literary ideas, but the creation out of discordant materials of a poetic symbol that stands for his mythic and poetic ideal of English history, and finally for his ideal of a harmonious and Edenic world. The ultimate problem of reconciliation of opposites in the two poems is similar; but subject, method, and viewpoint are different, and stylistically the result is a contrast.

The norm couplets employ a straightforward parallelism whose most distinctive feature is its compounding of verbs and predicates and less frequently of subjects and

objects. The syntax of the couplet norm is even simpler
and more straightforward than that of the *Pastorals*; but
it neither employs figures of rhetoric nor tricky balances
to the same extent, and it has a rich flowing quality that
surges beyond the closed couplet and sweeps all before it.
A key passage at the beginning of the poem expresses the
controlling theme of *concordia discors*, and shows how
skillfully Pope can suggest "harmonious discord" and
still maintain the forward movement and agreeing parallelism of his couplet norm:

> Here Hills and Vales, the Woodland and the Plain,
> 2 Here Earth and Water seem to strive again,
> Not *Chaos*-like together crush'd and bruis'd,
> 4 But as the World, harmoniously confus'd:
> Where Order in Variety we see,
> 6 And where, tho' all things differ, all agree.
> Here waving Groves a checquer'd Scene display,
> 8 And part admit and part exclude the Day;
> As some coy Nymph her Lover's warm Address
> 10 Nor quite indulges, nor can quite repress.   (11–20)

In keeping with the theme of the passage, the antithesis
of the couplets asserts paradoxical agreement. In spite of
the antithetic pull of "differ–agree," "admit–exclude,"
and "indulge–repress," they are controlled by "tho,"
"part (partly)," and "nor quite," which make their oppositions ambiguous. So the antitheses are openly smil-
ing and playfully hesitant; there is no real opposition for
the couplets are caught between antithesis and agreement and are as much one as the other. The branches, as
they play with the sunshine, are raised to the human
level in the similitude of Nymph and lover as "she" is
caught between granting and refusing, a harmonious
confusion of repulsion and attraction that in

Windsor-Forest lies at the heart of all things. The easy flow of the parallelism allows us momentarily to glimpse the tension of the couplet design. There is just enough repetition of the same words in both sentences of the passage to pull the whole toward anaphora: "here" and "where" are repeated in the first six-line sentence; "here" is lapped over at the beginning of the second sentence, and then "part" and "nor quite" are repeated. The last couplet of each sentence (ll. 5–6 and 9–10) is a subordinate clause, and the last line of each is built of antithetic parallels whose marker words, "tho' all" and "nor quite," point and emphasize each antithesis in a slightly different manner; for prosodic variety, the first antithesis (l. 6) has two strong pauses and the last (l. 10) has one. There is just the slightest contrast between the lilting melody of the passage and its note of discordant meaning, and Pope's varied repetition of sense and structure gracefully suggests his "Order in Variety."

One is hardly conscious of balanced antithesis and what little there is figures most prominently in the first hunting scene (ll. 43–90) in which Pope depicts the tyranny of the Norman kings and their wanton violation of the ideal harmony that prevailed in the forest. There are not more than four or five crisply antithetic couplets in this whole section:

> The Swain with Tears his frustrate Labour yields,
> 2 And famish'd dies amidst his ripen'd Fields.
>
> (55–56)

> Both doom'd alike for sportive Tyrants bled,
> 4 But while the Subject starv'd, the Beast was fed.
>
> (59–60)

> But see the Man who spacious Regions gave
> 6 A Waste for Beasts, himself deny'd a Grave!
>
> Stretch'd on the Lawn his second Hope survey,
> 8 At once the Chaser and at once the Prey.   (79–82)

Antithesis is softened as in lines 2 and 8 in which the antithetic idea occurs in undivided lines where Pope slips antithesis into individual words, "famish'd–ripen'd," "starv'd–fed," "Chaser–Prey," rather than puts it in recoiling hemistichs as in the *Essay on Criticism*. The tendency of the couplet structure is to pull the meaning away from opposition and to mute antithesis with a straightforward syntax and with the agreeing parallelism of the enclosing passages. In *Windsor-Forest* Pope pulls the syntax of couplets antithetic in meaning toward the agreeing syntax of his couplet norm for a definite purpose.

A more elaborate parallelism characteristic of the poem occurs below, in which subordinate clause lines vary the straightforward, linear compounding of the couplet norm:

> Nor yet, when moist *Arcturus* clouds the Sky,
> 2 The Woods and Fields their pleasing Toils deny.
> To Plains with well-breath'd Beagles we repair,
> 4 And trace the Mazes of the circling Hare.
> (Beasts, urg'd by us, their Fellow Beasts pursue,
> 6 And learn of Man each other to undo.)
> With slaught'ring Guns th' unweary'd Fowler roves,
> 8 When Frosts have whiten'd all the naked Groves;
> Where Doves in Flocks the leafless Trees o'ershade,
> 10 And lonely Woodcocks haunt the watry Glade.
> He lifts the Tube, and levels with his Eye;
> 12 Straight a short Thunder breaks the frozen Sky.
> Oft, as in Airy Rings they skim the Heath,

14 The clam'rous Lapwings feel the Leaden Death:
  Oft as the mounting Larks their Notes prepare,
16 They fall, and leave their little Lives in Air.   (119–34)

The passage begins with four lines of simple, objective description and narration, and then is jarred slightly by the antithetic aphorism in which the animal world becomes a destructive analogue of human aggression. In lines 7–10, the pairs of epithets work unobtrusively in undivided lines. The sentence is loose rather than periodic, and the subordinating "when" and "where" soften the rigid parallel epithets. "Naked Groves," "leafless Trees," "lonely Woodcocks," and "watry Glade" cohere to create a quiet, wintry vignette. But lurking behind the doves and woodcocks is the unwearied fowler, and suddenly the serenity of the wintry sky is shattered by the blast of the gun. The "clam'rous Lapwings" "skim" in "Airy Rings" and are brought down by the contrasting "Leaden Death," prosodically a heavy phrase. And in the final couplets the contrast between the fallen larks and the airy quality of the life that imaginatively continues in the suddenly vacated air above is nicely done. The pleasant, pictorial quality of the passage as a whole tends to pull the reader away from the discordant but necessary fact of slaughter and destruction.

A characteristic of this passage, which becomes a weakness in other places in the poem, is the too frequent occurrence of the trochaic adjective-noun pair—"leafless Trees," "watry Glade," and so on. Geoffrey Tillotson points out that we must look to Virgil to understand the reason behind the abstract, generalizing adjectives and epithets characteristic of eighteenth century pastoral and Georgic.[5] Nineteenth century readers grew to despise the

kind of epithets associated with the "poetic diction" of
the eighteenth century, especially such hackneyed puffs
as "scaly breed," "plumy race," "denizens of the trees,"
and so on. In the *Georgics* Virgil uses a similar form of
epithet and succeeds in compressing a vital and universal
poetic quality.[6] Renaissance poets, Spenser for one, had
used the Virgilian epithet with success, but in the eighteenth century its use hardened into a stilted and imitative formula.

Since Pope's influence was dominant during most of
the century, he easily became for later poets, especially
Wordsworth, the symbol of all they thought artificial in
Augustan poetic diction. In the preface to the *Lyrical
Ballads*, for example, Wordsworth damns Pope for his
poetic diction and later praises James Thomson for writing the best natural description since Milton. Wordsworth's animus was somewhat misdirected, however, for
it was Thomson who used much more of the kind of
diction Wordsworth revolted against than Pope. A comparison of *The Seasons* with any of Pope's poems later
than *Windsor-Forest* will convince even a casual reader
that Pope's epithets are not as wildly abundant or euphemistic as Thomson's. Pope, whose epithets are fresher
than those of most of the other poets of his time, refers
to the sun in the *Pastorals* and *Windsor-Forest* as
"Phoebus," or "Phoebus' fiery Car"; but in the *Rape of
the Lock* as simply "the Sun," or with mock-heroic fa-
miliarity as "Sol"; and after *Windsor-Forest*, fish are
never again the "Scaly Breed." Clearly Pope used too
many empty and ornate epithets in *Windsor-Forest*.
Frequently, though, he handles them with taste and
skill. They aid the smoothly structured parallelism distinctive of the poem helping to create, as in the passage

above, a generalized pictorial quality that supports Pope's method of description which contains symbolic as well as realistic value.

A form of parallelism used several times, and one which pares down the straightforward syntax of the couplet norm, is Pope's lists or catalogues. Pope introduced the catalogue of parallels in *Windsor-Forest* and used it later with telling effects in the *Rape of the Lock* and in the satires because of its capacity for the jolting parallelism of dissimilar ideas, but in *Windsor-Forest* it is used for a different thematic purpose. Following is a short scene from the second hunting episode, one of Pope's descriptions of the hunt as it was practiced in the reign of Queen Anne, which is the obverse of the tyrannical "man hunting" of the Norman kings. The pheasant has just been brought down by the hunter's gun, our "unweary'd Fowler" of a few lines back:

> See! from the Brake the whirring Pheasant springs,
> 2 And mounts exulting on triumphant Wings;
> Short is his Joy! he feels the fiery Wound,
> 4 Flutters in Blood, and panting beats the Ground.
> Ah! what avail his glossie, varying Dyes,
> 6 His Purple Crest, and Scarlet-Circled Eyes,
> The vivid Green his shining Plumes unfold;
> 8 His painted Wings, and Breast that flames with Gold?
> (111–18)

The couplet structure appears to be completely lacking in strategy, almost a mere listing in parallel verb phrases and direct objects, but Pope's playing of verbs and adjectives against nouns is more rewarding than it appears. The richly descriptive parallels are climactic and the last couplet achieves a fine emphasis. The verb governing the

list of nouns beginning in line 5 is "avail"; the order of
the first line of the last couplet (7) is inverted to enable
Pope to use the verb "unfold," with its suggestion of
continuant action, upon "vivid Green." The last line
follows with "painted Wings," then with the noun
"Breast," which is followed by a relative clause that puts
the emphasis not upon "golden breast" or the adjectival
quality of gold, but upon the noun function of "Gold"
in "flames *with* Gold." This is a nice contrast with the
verb "unfold" of the preceding line. The ordered lines
create a vivid impression, as the pheasant, fluttering in
blood and beating the ground with his wings, is caught
in the sacrificial act of unfolding his flaming colors.

Another passage of almost identical structure lists the
different kinds of fishes that Windsor Forest yields:

> Our plenteous Streams a various Race supply;
> The bright-ey'd Perch with Fins of *Tyrian* Dye,
> The silver Eel, in shining Volumes roll'd,
> The yellow Carp, in Scales bedrop'd with Gold,
> Swift Trouts, diversify'd with Crimson Stains,
> And Pikes, the Tyrants of the watry Plains.   (141–46)

A colorless verb, "supply," governs the catalogue of
nouns which are described in the briefest generality. But
the silver eel in "shining Volumes roll'd" is a vivid image
that catches the essence of the squirming, rolling eel.
Because the participle "roll'd" is the rhyme word, the
verb quality of "rolling" is emphasized rather than an
adjectival or substantive quality. "Shining Volumes" is
more effective coming before the rhyme "roll'd" than it
would be after it, for it is the climactic rolling or writh-
ing that is highlighted. We do not always think of
volumes as round but here it means "coils"; and when

"roll'd" describes "Volumes," the eelish effect is heightened, as the reader can easily imagine, even if he has never landed an eel. In the next line we find the yellow carp, then his scales, and last, their most striking quality, "bedrop'd with Gold." Finally it is fitting that the "Crimson Stains" of the trout come just before the tyrant pikes since both together suggest blood and conquest, and thus Pope reveals thematic purpose in a mere parallel list, for fish like men must have their tyrants.

The passages above on the pheasant and the fishes are effective not because of striking details, but because of the appropriateness of their concrete generality to their thematic progression. Such catalogues concentrate and order generalized particulars; and if Pope's description is brief and general, it is a generality that in Johnson's words does not "number the streaks of the tulip" but exhibits "such prominent and striking features as recall the original to every mind." The pheasant's breast that flames with gold is of no avail against the hunter's gun; the pheasant must die that men may not kill each other. The sacrificial gold of the pheasant's breast is absorbed into Pope's other uses of gold, which are frequently associated with a golden age of both past and future. The catalogue of fishes, luscious and tempting to the angler, ends with "Pikes, the Tyrants of the watry Plains," which have their analogue in tyrants of the terrestrial plains (like William the Conqueror and William III).[7] And in a similar catalogue of the tributaries and sons of Father Thames, the River Darent is stained with human blood like that larger entity for which it is a synecdoche, the history of Great Britain (340–48). Thus the catalogues with their rapid and general strokes of description suggest not only the color and variety of a real forest, but

the larger analogical relations of the forest to human
history and morality. The hunting and fishing scenes
comprise Pope's instance of well-accorded strife through
which men release their warlike and destructive energies
peacefully; and it is to this "peaceful strife" that Pope
refers later in Father Thames' prophesy of a peaceful and
productive England where arms are "employ'd on Birds
and Beasts alone" (374).

In the vision and prophecy of Father Thames
(355–423), Pope employs the straightforward multipli-
cation of predicates and clauses in open, suspended lines
characteristic of a rapt prophetic mode of speech; and
the varied syntax and sentence forms appropriate to an
argumentative and conversational poem, such as the
Essay on Criticism, are totally missing. Toward the end
of the vision, Pope's repetition of similar parallels speeds
up slightly and the poem seems to grow more vehement.
The following excerpt illustrates the compounding pattern of this mood, which recalls the method of Pope's
Messiah, which in turn reflects the linear, repetitive sentence structure of the prophetic verses of *Isaiah*, upon
which Pope's *Messiah* is partly based:

> For me the Balm shall bleed, and Amber flow,
> 2 The Coral redden, and the Ruby glow,
> The pearly Shell its lucid Globe infold,
> 4 And *Phoebus* warm the ripening Ore to Gold.
> The Time shall come, when free as Seas or Wind
> 6 Unbounded *Thames* shall flow for all Mankind,
> Whole Nations enter with each swelling Tyde,
> 8 And Seas but join the Regions they divide;
> Earth's distant Ends our Glory shall behold,
> 10 And the new World launch forth to seek the Old.
> (393–402)

The design of this is crystal clear, of course, but Pope's ellipsis skillfully aids his rhetorical emphasis. In the first two-couplet sentence, he suppresses after the first line, "for me . . . shall"; and in the second sentence, beginning with line 5, "The Time shall come, when. . . ." By themselves, the last two couplets are closed and complete in meaning, but incomplete with respect to the whole passage; they are but completions for "The Time shall come, when . . ." four lines back. As a result, Pope emphasizes more cleanly the verbs and objects, things and their actions, and invests the vision of Father Thames with color and grandeur. The antithesis of "join" and "divide" amid the parallels nicely recalls the theme, but the emphasis is clearly union rather than division; and the passage suggests that it is the business of men, through benevolence and justice, to join what nature, as well as evil men, have put asunder.

Father Thames's vision continues in the rhapsodic invocation of Peace, with an additional subtlety in the anaphorial parallels:

> Oh stretch thy Reign, fair *Peace!* from Shore to Shore,
> Till Conquest cease, and Slav'ry be no more:
> Till the freed *Indians* in their native Groves
> Reap their own Fruits, and woo their Sable Loves,
> *Peru* once more a Race of Kings behold,
> And other *Mexico's* be roof'd with Gold.   (407–12)

The mounting parallels change direction in the last couplet by employing two new subjects, "Peru" and "Mexico." The undivided lines of the last couplet close the sentence swiftly, and Pope gains dimension by playing an active verb against a passive—"Peru . . . behold"

against "Mexico's be roof'd." Peru deserves to see another race of her own kings; and justly Pope's line returns
the corrupting, stolen gold to the Indians of Mexico who
were robbed.

The couplet norm of *Windsor-Forest*, from which
Pope varies very little, is strongly dominated by agreeing
parallelism (as distinguished from antithetic). The frequent occurrence of color words, especially green and
gold, describes in an ideal way the actual forest, suggests
the archetypal vanished Eden, and points forward to a
new golden age. When such imagery is carried by the
compounding parallelism of the poem, the result is the
distinguishing texture and emotional tone of the poem:
a colorfulness and richness both in the closed and open
couplets, and a mounting vehemence sustained especially in the second half by frequent sweeps of open
couplets. Pope's lines have a forward, linear motion without the qualifiers and subordinations of his later poems;
and the resulting unity of couplet design, diction, and
imagery creates a friezelike poem which images not only
the poet's ardent wish for a new Eden, but also his vision
of the beauty of the actual world as it exists according to
the law of *concordia discors* and the principle of divine
analogy. But discord is present, as we have seen in the
details of the scenes, so Pope mutes antithesis in the
couplet structure, letting it emerge now and then, and
just enough to suggest the necessary theme of discord,
but not enough to break the serenity of his vision. The
couplet norm of the poem—sweeping, compounding
parallelism which sometimes picks up and blends antithetic structures into the flowing parallelism—is the
carrier of the poet's vision and a technique of harmonizing the diverse scenes out of which it came.

NOTES

1. Earl R. Wasserman, *The Subtler Language* (Baltimore: The Johns Hopkins University Press, 1959), pp. 101–68.

2. *Ibid.*, p. 103.

3. *Ibid.*, p. 129.

4. Introduction to *Windsor-Forest, Twick. Ed.*, I (1961), 133. Also Earl R. Wasserman, "Nature Moralized: The Divine Analogy in the Eighteenth Century," *English Literary History*, XX (1953), 39–76.

5. Geoffrey Tillotson, "Eighteenth-Century Poetic Diction," *Eighteenth Century English Literature, Modern Essays in Criticism*, ed. James L. Clifford (New York: Oxford University Press, 1959), pp. 212–32, *passim*.

6. *Ibid.*, *passim*.

7. Wasserman, *op. cit.*, p. 111.

5

ठ

The Rape of the Lock 1714

THE COUPLETS OF *The Rape of the Lock* brilliantly climax all of Pope's earlier couplet structures, but this triumph of style had to clear several obstacles. Because the poem "imitates" a real occurrence, employs complex satirical viewpoints, and offers a criticism of life, Pope's task was formidable indeed. Nor did his challenge to himself end here. Within the framework of the tiny plot, he chose to paint in some detail a picture of fashionable society, and to allude in almost every couplet to the great epics and to other literature as well.[1] The scope of the illusions is vast and pulls against the trivia of the plot. An engaging story had to be told within a complex literary, as well as actual, situation. To relate the humorous incident of the "rape," to paint the victim as a beautiful girl slightly flirtatious and amoral, and to underlay the rather wicked gaiety of the poem's surface with serious wit and morality, required a couplet strategy of the highest poetic order. Under such conditions an overemphasis of action or theme, the misuse of a particular stylistic mode, or an error of tone, could have been disastrous. Unless all these hazards were surmounted with clarity and delicacy, the poem would have lacked the exquisite balance of disparate elements which makes it the supreme example of mock epic, and which makes it, also, a poem of lasting interest and significance.

In addition to balancing and fusing these different aspects of his story into a work that engages the reader from beginning to end, Pope was writing about real people whose feelings he apparently did not wish to wound. To keep them in humor (which he failed to do), and to play back and forth upon the varied materials and themes of the story, Pope unified the narrator's viewpoint by holding a light and brilliant tone. For the purpose of his deeper satire, his couplets in many instances had to mean what they said on the surface, and then mean something else. The suggestive, double-edged implications of the couplets bear this out: they go beyond their face value or denotations to create ambiguities and *double entendre*. Nor could Pope, on the other hand, reveal himself as narrator to be openly lyrical, or sad, or too tender or concerned about his heroine or his theme, without a disconcerting change of tone. He therefore fashioned couplets of a tightly controlled unity of timbre but of great subtlety of structure and design.

I

Although balance and witty effects with zeugma and chiasmus abound in *The Rape of the Lock,* most of the couplets exhibit no conspicuous structural features. They fall into just about every syntactic pattern characteristic of the English sentence, but they have two or three common characteristics if no common structural patterns. They are simple; they employ a straight rather than a devious syntax; and they eschew structurally com-

lex subordinations. In this couplet majority, which is
the couplet norm, Pope avoids the brilliant balances he
uses in certain parts of the poem. Many of these norm
couplets appear to be syntactically innocent, but their
meanings may be anything but innocent. Many are used
for narration and exposition; and while they are fine
couplets—even fine poetry—they have little of the rich
ambiguity of other norm couplets of similar structure
but with different kinds of meaning than pure exposition
or narration. For example:

> Thrice rung the Bell, the Slipper knock'd the Ground,
> And the press'd Watch return'd a silver Sound.
> *Belinda* still her downy Pillow prest,
> Her Guardian *Sylph* prolong'd the balmy Rest.
>
>   (I. 17–20)

There is nothing deep or devious here. The reader must
be told that Belinda has a guardian and that it is he who
is prolonging her sleep. Clearly other things than structure give these lines their effect: a particular rhythm in
the first line where the caesura comes nicely on "Bell,"
then the quick second half of the line accords with the
quick action. In the second line Pope follows the first
two unaccented syllables with the spondee, "press'd
Watch," thus emphasizing the effort of the thing described. The spondee yields to the swift tripping iambics
of "return'd a silver Sound," where the alliteration working with the vowel sounds and with the falling sound
pattern of "Sound" helps to create almost a hypnotic
propriety of sound and action. The lines have a hushed
quality: we see and hear, but we don't want to wake up
Belinda—a trivial scene of a girl's bedroom, yet how

magically it is transformed within the strict limits of these four lines.

In the next example Ariel summons his Sylphs to guard Belinda:

> He summons strait his Denizens of Air;
> The lucid Squadrons round the Sails repair.
>
> (II. 55–56)

Here are two of the simplest sentences, yet, as in the first example, the sounds characterize things and actions. The couplet is dominated by eleven sibilants, suggestive in a general way of the silken, iridescent Sylphs. Here is another fine, simple couplet:

> But anxious Cares the pensive Nymph opprest,
> And secret Passions labour'd in her Breast.
>
> (IV. 1–2)

The rhyme reinforces the meaning, and "secret Passions labour'd" suggests Belinda's effort to hold her rage in check.

One can select couplets at random which are as direct as those above but whose syntax is more varied:

> Hither the Heroes and the Nymphs resort,
> To taste awhile the Pleasures of a Court.   (III. 9–10)

> But now secure the painted Vessel glides,
> The Sun-beams trembling on the floating Tydes.
>
> (II. 47–48)

And last, one whose structure is a little different from all those quoted above and whose sound system has a fine touch of grotesquerie:

> Behold, four *Kings* in Majesty rever'd,
> With hoary Whiskers and a forky Beard.
>   (III. 37–38)

The alliterations, "behold–hoary," "four–forky," and the "k" sounds in "Whiskers" and "forky" half-humorously and oddly describe the "Kings."

More than half the couplets in the poem are as direct and simple as these, and in most Pope gets the appropriate effect without any noticeable structural variation. But here, Pope's artistry with the simplest couplet begins to achieve a *tour de force* of witty ambiguity. While keeping syntactic directness and simplicity he achieves a crucially deepening significance with the couplet norm. For example, the fourth couplet of the opening of the poem asks this mock epic question:

> Say what strange Motive, Goddess! cou'd compel
> A well-bred *Lord* t'assault a gentle *Belle?*   (I. 7–8)

The syntax is uninvolved. What antithesis there is resides in the puzzlement about why a "well-bred *Lord*" would, of all things, "assault" not just any woman, but a "gentle *Belle*." The antithesis is between characters and action, not in any syntactic change of direction. The couplet starts a kind of deception with the high propriety of the invocation, then drops to its incongruous assault.

The parallels of the compound sentence below make a quick equation more surprising because of their ordinary structure:

> Now Lapdogs give themselves the rowzing Shake,
> And sleepless Lovers, just at Twelve, awake.
>   (I. 15–16)

Although the full meaning of the couplet is developed throughout the poem, the reader is met head-on by the ludicrous parallel. The couplet makes two apparently unrelated statements; but lovers get up at the same time as the dogs, so they must resemble them in some way.

When Ariel commands the Sylphs to guard the Virgin, Belinda, he emphasizes one particular duty:

> To fifty chosen *Sylphs*, of special Note,
> We trust th' important Charge, the *Petticoat*.
> (II. 117–18)

Pope takes advantage of the vertical binding of the rhyme to emphasize the issue at hand. We never again hear of the Sylphs of "special Note," but repeatedly of things related to petticoats. Not that anything happens to Belinda's petticoat literally; but the petticoat becomes a symbol of other things than a virginity which can be lost: good humor, moderation, and the traditional and age-old attributes of womanliness.[2] So the thing of "special Note" is, in fact, the petticoat.

Such couplets appear strategically throughout the poem. For instance in the first one below,

> *Belinda* now, whom Thirst of Fame invites,
> Burns to encounter two adventrous Knights,
> At *Ombre* singly to decide their Doom;
> And swells her Breast with Conquests yet to come,
> (III. 25–28)

it is clear that on the surface "Knights" means two young lords with whom Belinda wants to play cards. The pun on "Knights," though it is Pope's and not Belinda's, and the amatory suggestion of "burns" is Pope's hint that

Belinda is using the card game for a deeper purpose. And
what Belinda plays is of course Ombre, or "man."

Quite a lot of Pope's couplets hint unexpressed purposes which are part of the sexual game played in *The
Rape of the Lock*. Again in the game of Ombre, that
sinister contest of alternate glitter and shade, sexual conquest is hinted, and this couplet continues the seductive
implications of the card game:

> An *Ace* of Hearts steps forth: the *King* unseen
> Lurk'd in her Hand, and mourn'd his captive *Queen*.
> (III. 95–96)

The effect of stealthiness in this couplet is brought off by
no recoil of line or hemistich, but by two quiet words,
"unseen" and "lurk'd," one unambiguous and the other
with a double meaning, and also by a slight device of
line structure. The first half-line is bold and declarative;
the syntax of the next clause is similar, but the reader, by
means of the run-on line, skims into the sinister verb,
"lurk'd," which characterizes the deeper, real purposes of
the players.

After Belinda has lost her lock to the Baron's fraud,
she makes a classic Freudian slip of the tongue:

> Oh hadst thou, Cruel! been content to seize
> Hairs less in sight, or any Hairs but these!
> (IV. 175–76)

In the context of the poem one must extend the surface
meaning of this couplet. At this crucial moment Belinda
faces a dilemma, and the *double entendre* fits the deceptive sexual punning that occurs throughout. In keeping
with the psychological fall of losing her temper and

capitulating to her frivolous vanity, she has at last chosen the appearance of virginity instead of its reality. But paradoxically the couplet expresses another hidden wish in conflict with the first one, the wish to give herself to the Baron and fulfill herself as woman.

The epic, ringing couplet below carries in its unobtrusive subordinate clause one of Pope's most famous puns:

> Nor fear'd the Chief th' unequal Fight to try,
> Who sought no more than on his Foe to die.
>
> (V. 77–78)

The syntax is as innocent as that of the expositional couplets examined earlier. Naively it puts "try" and "die" in rhyme position, carrying the pun upon "die," which expresses the Baron's amatory purpose toward his "Foe," Belinda.[3]

The same opposition of the literal and symbolic occurs when Belinda draws her bodkin upon the Baron in the epic scuffle:

> Boast not my Fall (he cry'd) insulting Foe!
> Thou by some other shalt be laid as low.
>
> (V. 97–98)

The Baron's surface meaning is perhaps limited to the rude little contest going on in the elegant surroundings of Hampton Court, but Pope knows that he means more than what he says.

Throughout the poem the norm couplets, which carry much of the exposition and narration, take on a deepening significance when they carry the poem's motifs of concealment, seduction, and ironic surprise. They seem innocuous; but pun, ambiguity, and *double entendre* are more surprising and ironic in their straightforward syntax than in the parallels where we know quickly, in this poem at least, that Pope will more openly deal in ironic equations. The couplet norm deepens the appearance–reality theme in a strategic manner. One main aspect of reality in the poem—the underlying facts of courtship and sex which are bound up with the inexorable conditions of life—is less apparent, more subtle than the outward reality of social convention and custom which gives the poem much of its texture. The real motives of courtship, furthermore, are stronger but less conscious than the more artificial ones involved with the customs and fashions of a particular society. Thus in Pope's poem the norm couplets, which either steal, or leap, upon us with their hidden motives and irrepressible "facts of life," create a norm of meaning: Belinda's world of fashion, beautiful and yet sterile like the Sylphs who partly symbolize it, denies the deeper realities of sex and love which are sometimes inconvenient and which cannot be repressed without dire consequences to Belinda's real womanhood. The norm couplets express, even symbolize, this more real and deeper world.

II

The main variation against the couplet norm is the type of balance and parallelism so characteristic of Pope. Although balance is Pope's favorite structure in his earlier poems, it works in none of them with the rapier effects flashed in *The Rape of the Lock*. A favorite passage for commentators and teachers, and one typical of Pope's balanced mode, is the "epic warning" in which

Ariel tells the Sylphs of the "black Omens" threatening
Belinda:

> This Day, black Omens threat the brightest Fair
> 2 That e'er deserv'd a watchful Spirit's Care:
> Some dire Disaster, or by Force, or Slight,
> 4 But what, or where, the Fates have wrapt in Night.
> Whether the Nymph shall break *Diana's* Law,
> 6 Or some frail *China* Jar receive a Flaw,
> Or stain her Honour, or her new Brocade,
> 8 Forget her Pray'rs, or miss a Masquerade,
> Or lose her Heart, or Necklace, at a Ball;
> 10 Or whether Heav'n has doom'd that *Shock* must fall.
> (II. 101–10)

The music of the verse contains no dissonance but the
meaning does. The chiastic contrast of active and passive
in the third couplet (5–6) and the brilliant differenta-
tions of the rhyme contrasts have been ably commented
on by Wimsatt.[4] Pope's antithetic wit plays off important things against trivial things, a technique that drives
home the contrasts, for in the Sylphic world, honor and
brocade, heart and necklace are all equal. The progression of the rhymes emphasizes the helter-skelter atmosphere of Belinda's danger, and the balances trip through
a significant medley of things in Belinda's world. The
allusion to the marmoreal, remote classical purity of
Diana, which opens the world of things, finally comes to
an incongruous end in "Shock," Belinda's little hairy
lapdog. The passage illustrates a dimension of mock heroic that goes beyond mere convenient allusion; for sex
and love are no mere excuse for pun and fun, but are
fused with the texture and theme of the poem.

A second type of parallelism different from the sharply

balancing kind above, is more expansive and flowing, and
usually deals in irony or mock heroic. The design of the
following passage, in swelling heroics, immortalizes the
Baron's triumph, and at the same time dissolves its foun-
dation:

> While Fish in Streams, or Birds delight in Air,
> Or in a Coach and Six the *British* Fair,
> As long as *Atalantis* shall be read,
> Or the small Pillow grace a Lady's Bed,
> While *Visits* shall be paid on solemn Days,
> When numerous Wax-lights in bright Order blaze,
> While Nymphs take Treats, or Assignations give,
> So long my Honour, Name, and Praise shall live!
>
> What Time wou'd spare, from Steel receives its date,
> And Monuments, like Men, submit to Fate!
> Steel cou'd the Labour of the Gods destroy,
> And strike to Dust th' Imperial Tow'rs of *Troy*;
> Steel cou'd the Works of mortal Pride confound,
> And hew Triumphal Arches to the Ground.
> What Wonder then, fair Nymph! thy Hairs shou'd feel
> The conqu'ring Force of unresisted Steel?   (III. 163–78)

The parallels which yoke two natural creatures, birds and
fish, to British ladies make a satiric equation. Belles
accept the ephemeral world of fashion with its coaches
and sixes, silly romances, treats and visits, as unthink-
ingly as a bird the air; but if they were to really think,
they might not. So the Baron's empty triumph will live
forever even though the persons who immortalize it are
creatures of fashion: vanity is immortal. Pope is careful
not to overwork this structure, for in the second half at
line 9 he contrasts the subordinating parallels with a
surge of ringing declarations, and the spears of Achilles
and Ajax yield to the Baron's scissors, and Trojan towers
and Roman arches to Belinda's lock. The fallen lock was

an "imperial" monument, but a work of "mortal Pride," and like the towers of Troy, was felled by steel. Parallel subordinate lines in the first half give way in the second half to parallel predicates governed by the repeated subject "Steel," which acquires increasingly impressive force as the double predicates in each couplet reiterate the mighty works it has brought low. And Pope achieves a tremendous but appropriate waste of energy by concluding a series of destructions with the application of Freudian scissors in a half haircut.

Pope can hold the mock heroic tone and at the same time make his parallels forward the narration and maliciously reveal the character of the speaker. The meddlesome Thalestris has been urging Belinda to demand the return of the stolen lock, and as a last resort epically warns her that her reputation will be lost if she does not retrieve it:

> Methinks already I your Tears survey,
> Already hear the horrid things they say,
> Already see you a degraded Toast,
> And all your Honour in a Whisper lost!
>
> (IV. 107–10)

The modulating ellipses of these lines move to the climax in the last, where words have been increasingly dropped out until "Methinks already I . . . see" is cut entirely from the last line, but the satiric point Pope makes is that Thalestris "sees," not "hears," as she should, Belinda's honor lost in whispering gossip. The concision afforded by zeugma brings the passage to a sharply focused close, since all the words that remain after the ellipsis become progressively more important. The zeugma verb "see" achieves more than its denotation by implying an ambiguous relationship between the different actions it brings about—"degraded Toast" and "Honour in a Whisper lost." Such parallelism, therefore, has a power of implication that breaks the bounds of the couplet's pared-down concision.

III

Balance and parallelism, the main variation which we have examined above, is itself varied in several places by a similar mode which achieves a different purpose. This mode is thick with conspicuous nouns. It resembles the lists in *Windsor-Forest* but is less static, employs a controlling grammar which imparts movement to the things listed, and achieves livelier effects. For want of a better term, it can be called "noun cluster parallels." A typical example is this menuetto-like parade, which occurs within the fancy of a nymph too proud of her beauty to fall in love:

> Then gay Ideas crowd the vacant Brain;
> 2 While Peers and Dukes, and all their sweeping Train,
> And Garters, Stars, and Coronets appear,
> 4 And in soft sounds, *Your Grace* salutes their Ear.
> (I. 83–86)

The pompous little procession manages to reach its climax in the following manner. The names of the orders of knighthood in the two middle lines receive a sharper and more deliberate iambic emphasis than the first and last lines. The iambs dip and sway through the second and third lines till the rhythmic change of the last line with its soft sounding prepositional phrase, its sibilants and vowels, and its unctious salutation, "Your Grace," contrast the syntax and the tripping stopped consonants of the names of the orders. The first three lines reflect the pomp and glitter of the orders as the nymph fancies them, and the last line, her silken obeisance to them.

Here is a passage somewhat similar but more complex structurally and with a different kind of climax. This is the epic review of the "troops" at the beginning of the game of Ombre. The cards have been dealt:

> Behold, four *Kings* in Majesty rever'd,
> With hoary Whiskers and a forky Beard;
> And four fair *Queens* whose hands sustain a Flow'r,
> Th' expressive Emblem of their softer Pow'r;
> Four *Knaves* in Garbs succinct, a trusty Band,
> Caps on their heads, and Halberds in their hand;
> And Particolour'd Troops, a shining Train,
> Draw forth to Combat on the Velvet Plain. (III. 37–44)

First, the system of modification is different from that of the preceding passage. This one is slower because the nouns have modifying prepositional phrases and appositives. The "parade of the orders" passage trips in a direct and stately manner to its end, but the cards passage slows down for the mock epic build-up. The reader is told to behold, as Kings, Queens, Knaves, and the particolored troops pass in review, until at last the verb "draw" suddenly appears emphatically in the first position and throws the cards into combat formation.

Almost at the end of the poem, the lock ascends to the lunar sphere, a repository of things important in Belinda's world:

> There Heroes' Wits are kept in pondrous Vases,,
> And Beaus' in *Snuff-boxes* and *Tweezer-Cases*.
> There broken Vows, and Death-bed Alms are found,

And Lovers' Hearts with Ends of Riband bound;
The Courtier's Promises, and Sick Man's Pray'rs,
The Smiles of Harlots, and the Tears of Heirs,
Cages for Gnats, and Chains to Yoak a Flea;
Dry'd Butterflies, and Tomes of Casuistry.   (V. 115–22)

Pope makes the most of these balanced pairs of things,
for the half-humorous equivalents do more than juxta-
pose "Tomes of Casuistry" and "dry'd Butterflies." Not
a less pleasantly odd effect is the procession of rather
abstract and general nouns marching hand in hand with
trivial, concrete ones. Also, some of the lines pun.
"Bound" is a pun and another is suggested in the rhyme
of "Heirs" with "Pray'rs." A sick man's prayers are as
futile as the tears of disinherited heirs, and are nothing
but "airs" to boot. The main thing the nouns have in
common is their insubstantiality, even the ponderous
"Tomes of Casuistry"; and the rigid order of the parallels
contrasts oddly the scatterbrained "coherence" of the
things listed.

IV

An examination of the couplet designs of *The Rape of
the Lock* would be incomplete unless other fine passages
which do not fit the scheme of norm and variation are
accounted for. In each of these Pope creates a distinctive
design composed of different structures. The kinds of
couplets we have found thus far occur frequently, as do
other structures too numerous for classification. Compared with passages in Pope's earlier poems, these which
follow make it clear that in *The Rape of the Lock* Pope
achieved maturity as a stylist. His modulations from one
particular structure or design to another, or from one

sentence form to another, show more ease and grace than in any of the earlier works. The four opening paragraphs of the poem will illustrate:

> What dire Offence from am'rous Causes springs,
> 2 What mighty Contests rise from trivial Things,
> I sing—This Verse to *Caryll*, Muse! is due;
> 4 This, ev'n *Belinda* may vouchsafe to view:
> Slight is the Subject, but not so the Praise,
> 6 If She inspire, and He approve my Lays.
>   Say what strange Motive, Goddess! cou'd compel
> 8 A well-bred *Lord* t'assault a gentle *Belle?*
> Oh say what stranger Cause, yet unexplor'd,
> 10 Cou'd make a gentle *Belle* reject a *Lord?*
> In Tasks so bold, can Little Men engage,
> 12 And in soft Bosoms dwells such mighty Rage?
>   *Sol* thro' white Curtains shot a tim'rous Ray,
> 14 And op'd those Eyes that must eclipse the Day;
> Now Lapdogs give themselves the rowzing Shake,
> 16 And sleepless Lovers, just at Twelve, awake:
> Thrice rung the Bell, the Slipper knock'd the Ground,
> 18 And the press'd Watch return'd a silver Sound.
> *Belinda* still her downy Pillow prest,
> 20 Her Guardian *Sylph* prolong'd the balmy Rest.
> 'Twas he had summon'd to her silent Bed
> 22 The Morning-Dream that hover'd o'er her Head.
> A Youth more glitt'ring than a *Birth-night Beau*
> 24 (That ev'n in Slumber caus'd her Cheek to glow)
> Seem'd to her Ear his winning Lips to lay,
> 26 And thus in Whispers said, or seem'd to say.
>
> (I. 1–26)

The first two paragraphs have the form and manner of an epic opening and invocation, but not of course, the content. The dominant parallelism of these twelve lines fuses the slight and the heroic. First the portentous opening line; then with the next line, the reader begins to

adjust his focus. Here follows no resounding names of
gods and heroes, but the ordinary ones of Caryll and
Belinda; and the first paragraph ends with a conditional
"if" balance that hints a suitable mock epic fib: the poet
hopes for Caryll's approval and Belinda's inspiration,
neither of which could matter much in the long run, for
he is aiming at better judges than Caryll; and his real
source of inspiration is the "idea" of the poem, not a
particular young belle. The third paragraph, employing
the norm couplets beautifully, dips into the narrative of
the poem. Unlike the previous lines, these contain no
inversion or balance; they glide smoothly and deceptively
over the ironic contrast of the sun with Belinda's eyes,
those eyes which try to eclipse the sun but fail. The
second couplet (15–16), bland and plain, makes two
simple independent statements of fact; but the oblique
parallels of the earlier lines have prepared us for a deeper
relationship between men and lapdogs than that of mere
time. The straight narration continues but without
ironic texture; line 17 picks up the rustle and tinkle of
Belinda's first awakening; and in lines 23–26 a qualifying
parenthesis, with the doubtful alternative predicates in
the last line, ends the paragraph on an ambiguous note,
appropriate to Belinda's shadowy perception of the
dream from which she will soon awaken.

A fine modulation of structure occurs in a memorable
passage mostly in norm couplets, but the passage employs a flowing parallelism touched with a noun cluster.
It is the "rites of Pride" ending the first canto where
Betty dresses the Goddess Belinda:

    Unnumber'd Treasures ope at once, and here
  2 The various Off'rings of the World appear;

From each she nicely culls with curious Toil,
4 And decks the Goddess with the glitt'ring Spoil.
This Casket *India's* glowing Gems unlocks,
6 And all *Arabia* breathes from yonder Box.
The Tortoise here and Elephant unite,
8 Transform'd to *Combs*, the speckled and the white.
Here Files of Pins extend their shining Rows,
10 Puffs, Powders, Patches, Bibles, Billet–doux.
Now awful Beauty puts on all its Arms;
12 The Fair each Moment rises in her Charms,
Repairs her Smiles, awakens ev'ry Grace,
14 And calls forth all the Wonders of her Face;
Sees by Degrees a purer Blush arise,
16 And keener Lightnings quicken in her Eyes.

(I. 129–43)

This passage shows how Pope varies the progression of compound elements, shifting from the two-clause compound sentences to swifter compounding predicates, and then to compound objects which are subjects of verbs. The result is a sense of movement from the more static process of arming the warrior with the things from her "magazine" to a sense of potential activity at the end.

The arming begins with the first ten lines, smooth sentences that point to products from far away places, all of which have converged upon Belinda's dresser, the "altar of pride." The fifth couplet (9–10) closes the first section simply and objectively except for the insertion of one little shocking word, "Bibles," in the otherwise congruous list.[5] The sixth and seventh couplets (11–14), a compound sentence, change the pace with rapid predicates whose verbs, "rises," "repairs," "awakens," "calls forth," "sees," create a sense of converging preparation. The objects of these verbs suggest the power and quality of what is being put on: "Arms," "Charms," "Smiles,"

"Grace," "Wonders." In the last couplet, Pope doubles the object of the verb "sees," and makes in turn each object the subject of a following verb: "sees–Blush–arise," and "Lightnings–quicken." The first five closed couplets slow down the sense and activity, holding attention upon gems, combs, pins, patches, and so on; then in line 12 the couplets break closure, and swelling verbs ready Belinda for the eventful day. The lightnings in her eyes is a strategic metaphor; for just a little later when she sallies forth upon the Thames, her conquering eyes are "bright as the Sun."[6]

The opening of the second canto follows, after the final four lines of the first canto, the passage above, but Pope describes Belinda's appearance upon the Thames in couplets distinctively different from those which armed the Goddess for the "fight." Belinda arming her beauty in her toilet is one thing; but now she is the conquering goddess whose strategy, beauty, and flaws are combined in couplets almost unmatched anywhere else in Pope for their scintillating balances. After launching her, Aeneas fashion, on the "bosom" of the river, he presents her:

> Fair Nymphs, and well-drest Youths around her shone,
> 2 But ev'ry Eye was fix'd on her alone.
> On her white Breast a sparkling *Cross* she wore,
> 4 Which *Jews* might kiss, and Infidels adore.
> Her lively Looks a sprightly Mind disclose,
> 6 Quick as her Eyes, and as unfix'd as those:
> Favours to none, to all she Smiles extends,
> 8 Oft she rejects, but never once offends.
> Bright as the Sun, her Eyes the Gazers strike,
> 10 And, like the Sun, they shine on all alike.
> Yet graceful Ease, and Sweetness void of Pride,

12 Might hide her Faults, if *Belles* had Faults to hide:
   If to her share some Female Errors fall,
14 Look on her Face, and you'll forget 'em all.   (II. 5–18)

The balances recoil and spring forward at the same time. The first couplet points up Belinda's glitter by a qualification in line 2 which makes her the sun and those around her planets that shine by reflecting her light. If the second couplet (3–4) meant what it said, it would be merely lively and crisp. "Sparkling Cross," however, is only the ornament of the real object of adoration which Jews and Infidels would gladly kiss, an instance of Pope's deft use of the outward ornament for the underlying reality to create a delicate but sinister atmosphere of moral ambiguity. In the third couplet (5–6), one word, "unfix'd," shatters the comparison of "Mind" to "Looks" and "Eyes," by setting up the destructive equation. The fourth couplet (7–8) is caught between antithesis and parallelism; the second half of each line is an antithetic qualification of the first half. Elements are antithetically balanced by "none–all" and "oft–never," but the meaning is not exactly antithetic. Belinda can reject, can extend favors to none, and never once offend because she extends a smile to everyone, and thus demolishes antithesis. In the fifth couplet (9–10), which has neat grammatical division without balance of meaning, the sun metaphor bursts through again. The couplet is not antithetic, it contains strict, literal parallels; yet the last word, "alike," which reinforces the literal parallelism, creates a destructive comparison in agreeing parallels: the flirt, suddenly like the sun, shines on all alike.

The last two couplets (11–14) turn from balances to

ambiguous conditionals. The poet is sceptical of Belinda's intentions (suggesting the Jew and Infidel of line 4), but in the last couplet this attitude gives way to the narrator's straightforward ringing declaration, which is, in spite of Pope's recognition of her faults, unconditional surrender to her beauty. The syntax of the couplets pulls simultaneously toward an agreeing parallelism on the surface, yet points to an underlying discrepancy and ambiguity of meaning. As we have seen all along, things are not what they seem, but Pope does not let us forget that the relations between the appearance and the reality are by no means neat or simple, as he turns in the last four lines, not without frustration, from scepticism to belief.

But not all of *The Rape of the Lock* is witty, and Pope's motives are by no means always ulterior. He sometimes employs description to add color and texture, never forgetting, however, that it has its distinctive bearing on the total meaning of the poem. In the next passage, the Sylphs have descended into the sails of Belinda's ship to offer their fairy and ineffectual protection. Sylphs after all are the spirits of deceased coquettes, and coquettes are beautiful:

> Some to the Sun their Insect-Wings unfold,
> 2 Waft on the Breeze, or sink in Clouds of Gold.
> Transparent Forms, too fine for mortal Sight,
> 4 Their fluid Bodies half dissolv'd in Light.
> Loose to the Wind their airy Garments flew,
> 6 Thin glitt'ring Textures of the filmy Dew;
> Dipt in the richest Tincture of the Skies,
> 8 Where Light disports in ever-mingling Dies,
> While ev'ry Beam new transient Colours flings,
> 10 Colours that change whene'er they wave their Wings.
>   (II. 59–68)

This passage is remarkable for the peculiar kind of activity it depicts. It employs many verbs—"unfold," "waft," "sink," "flew," "disports," "flings," "change," "wave," and several participles—"dissolv'd," "glitt'ring," "dipt," "ever-mingling." Of all these verbs, however, only "unfold," "flings," and "wave" take objects. All the others are verbs of motion, but they are intransitive and less active than the transitive verbs. After the first couplet, furthermore, the lines (except 5) form appositives (3, 6, 10), subordinate clauses (8, 9), an adjective phrase (7), and an absolute construction (4). The passage lacks straightforward movement; the combination of rather static sentence structure with intransitive verbs and participles creates a sense of shimmering activity, which, however, does not act upon anything. As a result, the couplet design aids Pope's characterization of the Sylphs as they hang glittering in the sails.

A humorous passage of eccentric design is the one in which Sir Plume rails at the Baron to return the lock:

> With earnest Eyes, and round unthinking Face,
> He first the Snuff-box open'd, then the Case,
> And thus broke out—'My Lord, why, what the Devil?
> Z——ds! damn the Lock! 'fore Gad, you must be civil!
> Plague on't! 'tis past a Jest—nay prithee, Pox!
> Give her the Hair'—he spoke, and rapp'd his Box.
>
> (IV. 125–30)

All that the structure of this shows is that Pope could write almost any kind of couplet in *The Rape of the Lock*. The vacuous pomposity of Sir Plume is revealed by his words and actions. Slipped in neatly, the ludicrous pun of the second line fits the stupidity of the knight. It is the kind of blatant pun a clever person might make at the expense of a stupid one. Be that as it may, the passage is one of the finest examples of Pope's skill in blending an outburst of vulgar slang into the tone and texture of the poem without distorting in the least the meter or the closed, end–stopped form of the couplet.

In this periphrastic passage a pinch of snuff flies to its apotheosis:

> But this bold Lord, with manly Strength indu'd,
> 2 She with one Finger and a Thumb subdu'd:
> Just where the Breath of Life his Nostrils drew,
> 4 A Charge of *Snuff* the wily Virgin threw;
> The *Gnomes* direct, to ev'ry Atome just,
> 6 The pungent Grains of titillating Dust.
> Sudden, with starting Tears each Eye o'erflows,
> 8 And the high Dome re-ecchoes to his Nose.
>   (V. 79–86)

Odd that manly strength should be subdued by the finger and thumb of a young lady. The precision suggested by "Finger and Thumb" is carried over into the next couplet. The over-careful circumlocution of the third line, "Just where the Breath of Life," is transferred into the next line where the inverted object, "Charge of *Snuff*," puts off the action so that the rhyme verb, "threw," gains a precision and emphasis that would not be possible in its natural order. The sixth line, a fine mock epic periphrasis for snuff, humorous yet exact, puts the descriptive prepositional phrase, "of titillating Dust," appropriately before the climactic couplet, which brings a sudden catharsis to all this mincing inflation; and with the aid of the pun in "Dome," the room resounds to the Baron's sneeze.

The design of the final paragraph is as direct and
simple as Pope ever gets; but like Marvell or Herrick, he
invests the inexorable truisms of life with freshness and
vitality:

>   Then cease, bright Nymph! to mourn thy ravish'd Hair
> 2 Which adds new Glory to the shining Sphere!
>   Not all the Tresses that fair Head can boast
> 4 Shall draw such Envy as the Lock you lost.
>   For, after all the Murders of your Eye,
> 6 When, after Millions slain, your self shall die;
>   When those fair Suns shall sett, as sett they must,
> 8 And all those Tresses shall be laid in Dust;
>   *This Lock*, the Muse shall consecrate to Fame;
> 10 And mid'st the Stars inscribe Belinda's Name!
>
>   (V. 141–50)

The oblique antithesis of "boast" and "lost" in the second couplet prepares for the subordinate parallels that
follow, which are resolved by the last, simple declarative
couplet. The antitheses of the second and third couplets
(3–6) create a rhythm of giving and taking, of gaining
and losing. This rhythm, one can say, has been a princi-
pal theme all along, appearing crucially in Clarissa's
speech (V. 9–34) where gaining womanhood by losing
gracefully to the man appears as a *leit motif*. The fine
antithesis, "When, after Millions slain, your self shall
die," passes smoothly through the next two parallel lines
into the cadence of the final couplet. Not only is the
rhythm of the close an apotheosis of the lock itself, but
of the mock heroic as well. The deeds of Aeneas, Diana,
Hector, and Berenice are rare, but the folly and frailty of
young women is universal. The incident has been fittingly immortalized, but not for its triviality. Belinda
suffered a psychological fall when she lost her temper,

and thus, for the time being, rejected the world of womanhood that Clarissa held out to her. But Belinda's fall is a "fortunate fall."[7] She could have accepted the rape, recognizing the real meaning of the Baron's overture; she was ready to capitulate to him anyway because Ariel saw the earthly lover lurking at her heart and for this reason gave up his protection and his interest in Belinda. But because she is too much Belle and not enough woman, she must "suffer" from the rape by exposing her vanity and making a fool of herself. But she has contacted the Baron in the game of Ombre, and he still "lurks" at her heart at the moment of the rape. In these closing lines, then, Pope can envision her final "fall" to the fullness of womanhood. Comic though the rape of Belinda's lock is, there is just a hint in these lines of the blending of comic and tragic. The verve and lightness of the timbre and tone has never faltered, layering a surface of harmonizing gaiety over the poem's irony. But the muse who consecrates the lock, as well as the poem to its honor, looks through serious eyes upon her fragile beauty. Pope's keen irony becomes compassionate, for life, after all, is brief. The brilliant poet who has been partly a critic and satirist of Belinda recognizes at this final moment his involvement and oneness with Belinda in the common fate of all. A few sheets of paper with their poetic testimonial to a lock that is now dust will be all that remains of either.

V

In summarizing the functions of Pope's stylistic modes we must not forget that a theme or meaning carried by a particular structural design does not exclude the fact that this same kind of theme or meaning may be expressed by a different design. Pope is an artist, not a mathematician; and while a particular couplet design is strongly characteristic of a certain theme, the same meaning may occur sometimes in other structures and designs. The following summary is not meant, therefore, to classify rigidly, but to state the dynamic pattern of Pope's couplet style for the whole poem. The simple structures of the couplet norm are an instrument of deception: when they employ wit, pun, and *double entendre*, they create a slightly sinister meaning of seduction and shock, which forms the main thematic undercurrent of the poem's radiant gaiety. More explicitly than the norm couplets, many of the balanced and paralleled ones add a dimension of antithetic contrast in which the confused, and apparently fortuitous, ironic relationships of things, and hence of values, in the world of the poem are reflected. The noun-cluster parallels suddenly gather up and emphasize at appropriate places the concreteness and multiplicity of *things* when a thematic use of such things is necessary. The longer individual passages, such as the last ones examined, combine and blend different structures into passages which reinforce or climax various themes, as the passage on the Sylphs suggests the beauty and fragility of belles, and as the give and take of the parallels in the final lines of the poem emphasizes, in contrast to the heroine's character and actions, a deeper theme of the unchanging conditions, and values, of life. Pope creates within the little mock epic plot a complex moral and social world in which Belinda's lightheadedness, vanity, and beauty are played against an implicit scheme of age-old values for comic as well as for deeper and more serious ironic effects.

Pope's art of couplet structure and design simultaneously expresses and reflects this poetic world. Perhaps,
ultimately, *The Rape of the Lock* is a lyric in mock epic
form.

NOTES

1. Geoffrey Tillotson's introduction to the poem in *Twick. Ed.* II,
is excellent on the literary and social background of the poem.

2. Clarissa's speech, Canto V. ll. 9–34, makes it clear that good
humor, and merit or virtue are the things a woman must value in the
long run, and that in the "game" of love, the woman sooner or later
must surrender, gracefully and with good humor, even though a man
has playfully snipped off a lock of her hair.

3. Cleanth Brooks' discussion of the pun on "die," and indeed of
the whole poem, lies in the background of my discussion of Pope's
puns and *double entendre*. See "The Case of Miss Arabella Fermor,"
The Well Wrought Urn (New York: Harcourt, Brace & World, Inc.,
1947), pp. 80–104.

4. *The Verbal Icon*, p. 162.

5. One of the felicities of this line is that the voiceless *p* sound continues throughout the line, merely changing to its voiced equivalent
b sound on the last two nouns, "Bibles" and "Billet-doux."

6. Although Belinda is indeed beautiful, her blush and her brilliant
eyes are partly the result of rouge and belladonna. See *Twick. Ed.* II,
pp. 155–56.

7. Aubrey Williams, "The 'Fall' of China and *The Rape of the
Lock*," *Philological Quarterly*, Vol. 41 (1962), pp. 420–21, 425.
Williams argues convincingly that Belinda's "fall" can be regarded, in
one sense, as a fortunate one into a "more natural human condition,"
and that, in addition to its wit and gaiety, the poem carries serious
meanings.

6

Eloisa to Abelard 1717

BETWEEN *The Rape of the Lock* and *Eloisa to Abelard* there is a radical difference of style. Missing in *Eloisa to Abelard* is the bright timbre and sparkling atmosphere, the brilliant interweavings of the several levels of the poem in a variety of couplet designs, and the rich, ambiguous viewpoint of the author toward his heroine, so compelling a feature of *The Rape of the Lock. Eloisa to Abelard* lacks the complex irony of the epic, social, and moral reticulation of Belinda's fall, but on the other hand it is told and experienced from the first person point of view; it is intense and passionate, and the concept upon which it is built—the opposition of body and soul—has been a central theme of western literature since the Greeks. Pope's poem is a distinctive variation upon this great theme. Its style is unique among Pope's major poems, unlike his earlier style which came to its fruition in *The Rape of the Lock,* and unlike the styles Pope employed when he resumed his "original" poetic career after the ten years spent translating Homer.

Pope rewrote the story of Eloisa and Abelard from John Hughes' translation of the letters of Eloisa to Abelard (1713), which was a free translation of Bussy's

French translation of the original Latin letters.[1] Pope did
not know either Eloisa's original Latin letters or the
French translation which Hughes used, so his poem, like
Plato's famous bed, is three times removed from its
source. The Eloisa Pope wrote about was romanticized
in Bussy's translation, and this romantic quality was re-
tained by Hughes.[2] Pope's Eloisa has popularly been
thought of as a romantic figure because her story is unusual and violent, because she loses control of her emotions, and because the setting and atmosphere of the
poem is gloomy and Gothic. If the poem is romantic, it
is not romantic in a popular sense, for many of Eloisa's
intense emotional responses to her conflict and to the
picturesque gloom of her environment are naturalistic.[3]
They have an immediate, practical, physical reason, and
are hardly those of a mind torn with the manic frenzy of
frustrated sexual passion. And though her passion is violent and unusual, it is not cut off from literary traditions,
as Geoffrey Tillotson points out:

> Pope's passion, then derives from Nature and Ovid
> (Nature and Ovid were, he found, the same) newly
> flushed with the experience of the time in France and
> England. But flushed, also, with Pope's own Roman
> Catholic devotion and the poetry of the mystics. It is
> significant that the debt to Crashaw, like that to Milton,
> reaches to the point of a line of quotation, a debt which
> is considered too odd to go unspecified. . . . It was this
> conflict between religious vows and paganism, between
> 'grace and nature, virtue and passion' which, for Cha-
> teaubriand, marked her superiority over any ancient her-
> oine. From the literary point of view the conflict is
> central: the poem is constructed around it. And it pro-
> vides opportunity for those 'layerings' of effect which are
> so characteristic of Pope's methods of writing. It allows
> the Ovidian imitation to be parallel and divergent at the
> same time.[4]

Tillotson points out in another place that Pope brings
the heroic epistle back to its strict Ovidian definition, for
the characters are historical and the woman abandoned
by her lover.[5] Pope, however, retains much of the general
character and atmosphere of Hughes' translation,[6] but
gives it, of course, the unique touch of his sensibility and
his couplet. The main difference between Pope's poem
and the two translations is that in Pope's poem the
conflict between Eloisa's religious vows and her love for
Abelard is more sharply focused. In his "Argument" to
the poem, Pope states what is really the idea or "plot"
which sets his work apart from all other versions of the
story:

> After a long course of Calamities, they retired each to a
> several Convent, and consecrated the remainder of their
> days to religion. It was many years after this separation,
> that a letter of Abelard's to a Friend which contain'd
> the history of his misfortune, fell into the hands of
> Eloisa. This awakening all her tenderness, occasion'd
> those celebrated letters (out of which the following is
> partly extracted) which give so lively a picture of the
> struggles of grace and nature, virtue and passion.[7]

Pope's poem is a synthesis of Hughes' translation of
Eloisa's letters. Abelard's letter, which is feigned by Pope
to have come suddenly into Eloisa's hands, provokes the
burst of battling emotions which is the poem. Pope perceived the drama which the whole unfortunate career of
Eloisa would make had it really been compressed by
Eloisa's single, overwhelming letter, which begins *in me-
dias res* and which climaxes and solves her inward conflict of nature and grace.

The source of the poem's conflict is Eloisa's inability,
or unwillingness, to renounce or purge an erotic fantasy
which invades and stains her love of God. Her bride-

groom should now be Christ, and her love for Abelard is in its present form adulterous. The conflict between nature and grace structures the poem according to the following pattern. In the first third of the poem (through line 117) Eloisa reviews the history of her life with Abelard and her subsequent career in the convent up to the time she opens Abelard's letter containing the history of the affair. His letter causes Eloisa's reply, which is, of course, the poem itself. For a while she is melancholy and restrained. The review and examination of her position, however, forces her to the brink of the abyss, her persistent amorous desire for Abelard; and she is driven to express her physical passion for Abelard, which she knows is wrong, and which prompts the expression of an equally fierce desire for the opposite, a state of grace or religious serenity. Before the end of the poem, she transforms her physical passion for Abelard into a state of religious ecstasy that envelops Abelard as priest and spiritual "lover." After her first outburst, when she cries out for Abelard's presence (119–28), her moods oscillate from her passionate desire for the *eros* she wants to remember, to the desire for the grace, or *agape* which she knows is her religious salvation. At one moment she desires Abelard as physical lover, in the next as spiritual lover and priest, or surrogate for Christ. As the oscillation of her moods grows shorter and more intense, and as the polarities of her struggle swing closer together, she finally envisions in death the resolution of her dilemma. The compulsive memory of Abelard as earthly lover will be transcended by her mystical union with him in heaven; and in renouncing Abelard as earthly lover, Eloisa can fulfill her marriage of "grace" with the mystical spouse Christ, and Christ includes all, even Abelard.[8]

Her choice is actually hell alone, or heaven with Abelard;
and her sacrifice to gain heaven is the renouncing of
desire for the earthly Abelard, which she accomplishes at
the end of the poem.[9] The cruel nature of her conflict is
that she really knows Abelard is committed to holiness
because he is sexually dead. The real object of renunciation, however, is not Abelard himself, but Eloisa's obses-
sion with the memory of his physical love and her
present desire for it, which is, of course, futile. Moreover
one of the poem's more general but compelling themes is
the strength and haunting torment of Eloisa's obsessive
memory of a love that usurps her present love of God,
and damns her future.

The setting of the poem and its atmosphere cooperate
in a rather unusual manner with Eloisa's passion. The
conflict which structures the poem goes on deep within
her mind, and her fierce inward struggle takes place in
the eerie half-light of the gloomy and silent convent.
Despite the vehemence of much of her language, the
reader sees and hears her violent emotions happening
within the still convent, and within the mind of the
outwardly controlled and severe nun. This silent, episto-
lary mode in the gloomy convent creates a dark, melancholy emotional coloring that dominates the poem; but
now and then, and at the end, the rhythm of her struggle
illuminates the melancholy atmosphere with her visions
of renunciation and union with God. The total visual
and sensuous effect of the action in its setting is a kind of
"darkness visible," with the light of religious ecstasy
piercing it intermittently.

Pope does not use a clear-cut couplet norm in this
poem, and with such a heroine as Eloisa the description
of the dominant couplet style grows more difficult. Quite

a few of the couplets of the first half contain balanced
antithesis and parallelism, which express Eloisa's more
reasoned, analytical attitude toward her conflict, but
Pope employs slightly less balanced antithesis than in
The Rape of the Lock, and considerably less than in the
Essay on Criticism. Taken altogether, the poem's couplets have a frequent periodic sentence form that emphasizes the last part of the couplet or sentence; this
periodic form creates more subordinate clauses than are
found in the earlier poems. Main sentence parts such as
subject, verb, or predicate are often repeated, which is
not customary with Pope, but the repetitions express
Eloisa's obsessive desire to relive and recapture her past.
Pope uses considerable inversion, but no more than in
The Rape of the Lock, as one can tell from a quick
scanning of the lines, but the inversions are more complex. For the most part, those of the preceding poem are
the ordinary ones characteristic of verse, like the simple
inversion of verb and object. But those of *Eloisa to
Abelard* are more compressed because more of the controlling and explicit grammar characteristic of the ordinary and traditional English sentence structure is omitted. Pope has made his heroine as much Roman and
Ovidian, as much French and Racinian, as English;
and the subtle debate of passion and virtue which gives
form to the sweeps of emotion owes something to Ra-
cine's Polyeucte and Bérénice, and more to Ovid's hero-
ines.[10] Thus, Pope's couplets frequently have a
wrought-iron compression and inversion more characteristic of Latin and French poetry than English.

Tillotson points out that Eloisa "pits one situation
against another, formalizes, makes points," and quotes

the following couplet as an example of what he calls Eloisa's "emotional geometry":[11]

> Nature stands check'd; Religion disapproves:
> Ev'n thou art cold—yet *Eloisa* loves.   (259–60)

It is true that Eloisa makes points and creates a kind of emotional symmetry based on the oppositions of nature and grace, as is shown further in these couplets:

> Back thro' the paths of pleasing sense I ran,
> Nor wish'd an Angel whom I lov'd a Man.   (69–70)

> I ought to grieve, but cannot what I ought;
> I mourn the lover, not lament the fault.
> I view my crime, but kindle at the view,
> Repent old pleasures, and sollicit new.   (183–86)

Here is Pope's familiar balanced antithesis, the oppositions Eloisa must fuse and transcend to attain a state of grace. We should notice also, before going on, that while these lines suggest the balances of the *Essay on Criticism*, Pope's ellipsis is more extreme and reflects the concision of French and Latin constructions. When Eloisa "thinks" or reasons, as in the couplets above, she states the oppositions of her conflict sharply; but her emotional change from sinful enslavement to human passion, to renunciation of earthly passion and union with God, has a different poetic quality than her antithetic analysis and description of the dilemma in which she is entangled. Her antithetic point-making is the intellectual aspect of her deeper emotional conflict, and the progression of her emotions dominates her antithetic couplets. A paragraph which contains more antithesis

than any other in the poem will make clear the nature of
this progression:

> Ah wretch! believ'd the spouse of God in vain,
> 2 Confess'd within the slave of love and man.
>   Assist me heav'n! but whence arose that pray'r?
> 4 Sprung it from piety, or from despair?
>   Ev'n here, where frozen chastity retires,
> 6 Love finds an altar for forbidden fires.
>   I ought to grieve, but cannot what I ought;
> 8 I mourn the lover, not lament the fault;
>   I view my crime, but kindle at the view,
> 10 Repent old pleasures, and sollicit new:
>   Now turn'd to heav'n, I weep my past offence,
> 12 Now think of thee, and curse my innocence.
>   Of all affliction taught a lover yet,
> 14 'Tis sure the hardest science to forget!
>   How shall I lose the sin, yet keep the sense,
> 16 And love th' offender, yet detest th' offence?
>   How the dear object from the crime remove,
> 18 Or how distinguish penitence from love?
>   Unequal task! a passion to resign,
> 20 For hearts so touch'd, so pierc'd, so lost as mine.
>   Ere such a soul regains its peaceful state,
> 22 How often must it love, how often hate!
>   How often, hope, despair, resent, regret,
> 24 Conceal, disdain—do all things but forget.
>   But let heav'n seize it, all at once 'tis fir'd,
> 26 Not touch'd, but rapt, not waken'd, but inspir'd!
>   Oh come! oh teach me nature to subdue,
> 28 Renounce my love, my life, my self—and you.
>   Fill my fond heart with God alone, for he
> 30 Alone can rival, can succeed to thee.   (177–206)

The first part of this paragraph, the first four lines, is an
outburst of despair ended by the question of line 4. The

second part, lines 5–12, is prompted by the question of line 4, and its series of parallels passes the antithesis of Eloisa's conflict swiftly before her mind; and here the antithesis in line 8–10 grows complex where "lover," "crime," and "pleasures" are constants, and Eloisa's shifting attitudes toward them comprise the antithesis. The third part, 13–20, continues the flow of antithesis begun in the previous lines, but they slow down; she grows baffled by the complexity of her dilemma, and in lines 19–20 gives up the more reasoned analysis of her struggle. In the fourth part, lines 21–24, the tension generated in parts two and three is climaxed by the weighty list of opposites and particulars which brings her to the despair of being unable to forget. Finally in the fifth part, lines 25–30, she drives her battling emotions, altogether as it were, toward unity and transcendence in God. Eloisa's debate, or dialectic, is, of course, the cause of the poem in the most real sense, but it is not her debate as such, nor her point making or "emotional geometry" that makes the most significant impact. Her antithetic statements about her conflict release powerful emotions, which are variously directed either toward Abelard or God. These sweeps of emotion either repel, or engulf and transcend antithesis and debate, and their movement creates the most compelling and dramatic aspect of the poem: the rhythm of Eloisa's divided will, which is her repeated struggle to break the fetters of an obsessive, erotic memory of physical passion, and to soar free from the prison of her earthly love.

A passage early in the poem illustrates the pervasive melancholy, hints the opposition of Eloisa's outer and inner worlds, and shows how the dominant couplet structures work. Eloisa looks around her at the rocks and walls of the convent, and contrasts her surroundings with the state of her mind:

> Relentless walls! whose darksom round contains
> 2 Repentant sighs, and voluntary pains;
> Ye rugged rocks! which holy knees have worn;
> 4 Ye grots and caverns shagg'd with horrid thorn!
> Shrines! where their vigils pale-ey'd virgins keep,
> 6 And pitying saints, whose statues learn to weep!
> Tho' cold like you, unmov'd and silent grown,
> 8 I have not yet forgot my self to stone.
> All is not Heav'n's while *Abelard* has part,
> 10 Still rebel nature holds out half my heart;
> Nor pray'rs nor fast its stubborn pulse restrain,
> 12 Nor tears, for ages, taught to flow in vain.   (17–28)

There is nothing unusual or torqued here as in the couplets of the *Essay on Criticism* and *The Rape of the Lock*. The first four lines employ three apostrophes completed by relative clauses which explain and characterize them; then in line 5, another apostrophe, "Shrines," and the line comes to something closer at hand for Eloisa, to "pale-ey'd virgins" keeping vigil. Lines 7 and 8, a fine example of Pope's concise, periodic couplet form, bring the rhetorical, rather static apostrophes and subordinate clauses to a climax with the bold and simple declaration of line 8, which suddenly reveals Eloisa's suffering in contrast to the ghostly shrines and marble statues. The last two couplets, like the statues, are carved in marble. The concise statement of line 9 ill accords with the confused passion which will be its result later on. The tightened concision of the last couplet, with the un-English use of "nor," ends with a grammatical anticlimax, "taught to flow in vain," which, nevertheless, throws a perspective of suffering and never ending sorrow upon the whole paragraph. The sound of the rhyme pattern suggests the emotional progression. The predominant nasals combined with long vowels which suggest a groan or moan yield in 5–6 and 9–10 to the contrast of stopped consonants with also a vowel contrast in 9–10; and with the last rhyme, the sound reverberates the meaning: "restrain–vain." The emotional movement of this paragraph is similar to the wavelike movement of others in the poem. There is a slight rise of Eloisa's emotions, restrained, however, by the static form of the apostrophes until "Shrines" (5), the crest of this upward movement. Then her feeling takes a different direction in a contrasting process and quietly subsides into the "stubborn pulse" and silent tears of the marmoreal nun. Later these emotional crests break violently. Although meaningless by itself, the sound of the passage supports the movement of its idea, from a melancholy situation with an objective reference to the slow pulsing of a hopeless passion.

The next paragraph shows further some features of the dominant structures, and also picks up one of the main variations. Eloisa recalls her taking of the vows; and the conflict of her unholy passion with the solemnity of the occasion motivates the expression of her desire for Abelard:

> Canst thou forget that sad, that solemn day,
> 2 When victims at yon altar's foot we lay?
> Canst thou forget what tears that moment fell
> 4 When, warm in youth, I bade the world farewell?
> As with cold lips I kiss'd the sacred veil,
> 6 The shrines all trembled, and the lamps grew pale:
> Heav'n scarce believ'd the conquest it survey'd,

8 And Saints with wonder heard the vows I made.
  Yet then, to those dread altars as I drew,
10 Not on the Cross my eyes were fix'd, but you;
  Not grace, or zeal, love only was my call,
12 And if I lose thy love, I lose my all.
  Come! with thy looks, thy words, relieve my woe;
14 Those still at least are left thee to bestow.
  Still on that breast enamour'd let me lie,
16 Still drink delicious poison from thy eye,
  Pant on thy lip, and to thy heart be prest;
18 Give all thou canst—and let me dream the rest.
  Ah no! instruct me other joys to prize,
20 With other beauties charm my partial eyes,
  Full in my view set all the bright abode,
22 And make my soul quit *Abelard* for God.   (107–28)

In the first couplet she lingers, repeating and varying a thought: "sad," "solemn"—sad to her, solemn in its more public aspect. The next couplet repeats "Canst thou forget" like a refrain, where she is compelled to hold on to the memory. Through line 11, the passage develops the objective and general features of the situation in a straightforward manner. She fixes her eyes upon Abelard rather than upon the bound and bleeding lover on the cross; in a previous paragraph (99–106) she had just envisioned Abelard's castration, calling him a "bound," "bleeding," "naked Lover." The image of Abelard and Christ is ironically interchangeable here; and in line 12 the lovers are confused again: it is, of course, Abelard's love that she speaks of, but in the truest sense, it is Christ's love that she must not lose by remaining enslaved to her memories of Abelard as earthly lover. Line 12 turns inward, and the accelerating verb phrases that follow express her desperate passion for Abelard as lover, but suddenly shift direction in line 19 to express her desire for Abelard as priest. This passage, the first one which confuses the two roles of Abelard as earthly lover and as priest, generates a pattern of ambivalent, oscillating passion which she cannot resolve until the end of the poem.

Sudden shifts of structure characterize Eloisa as she turns from one mode of expression to another:

> But why should I on others' pray'rs depend?
> 2 Come thou, my father, brother, husband, friend!
> Ah let thy handmaid, sister, daughter, move,
> 4 And all those tender names in one, thy love!
> The darksom pines that o'er yon' rocks reclin'd
> 6 Wave high, and murmur to the hollow wind,
> The wandring streams that shine between the hills,
> 8 The grots that eccho to the tinkling rills,
> The dying gales that pant upon the trees,
> 10 The lakes that quiver to the curling breeze;
> No more these scenes my meditation aid,
> 12 Or lull to rest the visionary maid.   (151–62)

In the first four lines she entreats Abelard in a series of nouns, her lowest common denominator of expression, as if naming her desires would cause them to materialize. Recognizing that her outburst is futile she modulates at line 5 to a passage of open parallels whose calm surface does not conceal their passion. As she projects her emotion upon the external world, even trees and lakes are invested with the semblance of human passion. In sharp contrast to the imperative verbs and nouns that she shrieks at other places, the parallels suggest the female passivity she wishes to enjoy with Abelard. In lines 9–10 "dying," "pant," "quiver," and "curl," imply the fulfillment she longs for. Lines 5–10 are composed of nouns followed by a subordinate "that" clause, plus verb and prepositional phrase, a rigid design whose repetitive structures without controlling verbs reflect a tense, trancelike mood as Eloisa deeply absorbs herself in the image making of the parallels. Realizing that this kind of absorption is hopeless, she suddenly gives the parallels grammatical resolution and closes. This periodic design, like others in the poem, has a formal quality similar to music, where a series of similar, and brief, suspended phrases are cadenced by a final phrase which comes to rest on the dominant chord.

The emotion created by the lines above contrasts Eloisa's emotion when she directs it to Abelard as physical lover, or to him as a surrogate for Christ in series of imperative short phrases or single words. This kind of feeling, which she makes objective by going outside her own direct willing for Abelard, is repeated twice more in similar designs, in her description of the serenity of the "blameless Vestal" (207–14) and of Abelard's spiritual calm for which she longs in vain:

> For thee the fates, severely kind, ordain
> 2 A cool suspense from pleasure and from pain;
> Thy life a long, dead calm of fix'd repose;
> 4 No pulse that riots, and no blood that glows.
> Still as the sea, ere winds were taught to blow,
> 6 Or moving spirit bade the waters flow;
> Soft as the slumbers of a saint forgiv'n,
> 8 And mild as opening gleams of promis'd heav'n.
>   (249–56)

The first line ends with the euphemistic but dignified Latinate verb, "ordain," which is a pun for castration and for taking the vows of priest. It is run-on and sets up a contrast with the static, absolute constructions of lines 3 and 4. The parallel lines 5 through 8 emphasize metrically the adjectives, "still," "soft," and "mild" while avoiding transitive verbs and active voice. In structure, in sound, and in sense, the passage suggests "fix'd repose." Nor is it sensational or vulgar. Eloisa, who suffers most at the moment from the implied act, expresses Abelard's, and consequently her own, deprivation with the utmost generality and delicacy, suggesting a kind of death and release from passion, for which, at the moment, she yearns.

The twenty lines following the last line in the passage above, make clear, when considered with the passage above, the rhythmic form of Eloisa's feeling. Having just seen Abelard as sexually dead, she begins with a slight taunt but is engulfed by the fiery phantoms of earthly love:

> Come *Abelard!* for what hast thou to dread?
> 2 The torch of V*enus* burns not for the dead;
> Nature stands check'd; Religion disapproves;
> 4 Ev'n thou art cold—yet *Eloisa* loves.
> Ah hopeless, lasting flames! like those that burn
> 6 To light the dead, and warm th' unfruitful urn.
> What scenes appear where-e'er I turn my view!
> 8 The dear Ideas, where I fly, pursue,
> Rise in the grove, before the altar rise,
> 10 Stain all my soul, and wanton in my eyes!
> I waste the Matin lamp in sighs for thee,
> 12 Thy image steals between my God and me,
> Thy voice I seem in ev'ry hymn to hear,
> 14 With ev'ry bead I drop too soft a tear.
> When from the Censer clouds of fragrance roll,
> 16 And swelling organs lift the rising soul;
> One thought of thee puts all the pomp to flight;

18 Priests, Tapers, Temples, swim before my sight;
    In seas of flame my plunging soul is drown'd,
20 While Altars blaze, and Angels tremble round.

                                          (257–76)

The first paragraph contains the antithetic point making noted by Tillotson, especially in lines 3–4. This couplet, however, is not like Pope's typical balanced couplet: it has no pivotal caesura, it lacks chiastic syntax, or meaning, and the negating climax overwhelms and cancels all three preceding statements. This is not really antithesis, which involves the opposition of equal things, but an incongruity of heroic love. Then she ends the paragraph in a couplet of slashing speed and directness filled with irony and paradox rather than antithesis. In lines 7–14 she describes the pursuing images of Abelard in almost neutrally structured couplets, simple and direct. In line 15 she begins building the climax. Even at mass, it is the love–image of Abelard that casts her into the flames of literal Hell rather than the image of Christ who should lift her to the seraphic state of the "blameless Vestal." She ends, rather unusually, in a subordinate clause which leaves the right impression: the blazing altars and trembling angels (statuary) are the things she sees through her tears as she imaginatively sinks downward in seas of flame.[12] Irony and incongruity define the situation, not antithesis, and the process of changing from one pole of emotion to another strongly dominates the antithetic couplets.

   At the end of her struggle, when she is undergoing the agonizing process of final renunciation, her expression is as fiercely amorous as before. As Geoffrey Tillotson observes, "Having made religion into an erotic experience, she ends by making death one, too":[13]

I come, I come! prepare your roseate bow'rs,
2 Celestial palms, and ever-blooming flow'rs.
Thither, where sinners may have rest, I go,
4 Where flames refin'd in breasts seraphic glow.
Thou, *Abelard!* the last sad office pay,
6 And smooth my passage to the realms of day:
See my lips tremble, and my eye-balls roll,
8 Suck my last breath, and catch my flying soul!
Ah no—in sacred vestments mays't thou stand,
10 The hallow'd taper trembling in thy hand,
Present the Cross before my lifted eye,
12 Teach me at once, and learn of me to die.
Ah then, thy once-lov'd *Eloisa* see!
14 It will be then no crime to gaze on me.
See from my cheek the transient roses fly!
16 See the last sparkle languish in my eye!
Till ev'ry motion, pulse, and breath, be o'er;
18 And ev'n my *Abelard* be lov'd no more.
O death all-eloquent! you only prove
20 What dust we doat on, when 'tis man we love.

(317–36)

The only difference between this design and that of other passages typical of her passion is that the sentences are longer, the staccato imperative nouns and verbs are missing, and the imperative clauses have taken over. Her passion, while still intense, is beginning to subside into longer rhythms, for its more turbulent physical aspect is moving toward transcendence. The next lines following the last above complete her vision of blissful fulfillment:

Then too, when fate shall thy fair frame destroy,
(That cause of all my guilt, and all my joy)
In trance extatic may thy pangs be drown'd,
Bright clouds descend, and Angels watch thee round,
From opening skies may streaming glories shine,
And Saints embrace thee with a love like mine.

(337–42)

For Eloisa death will be like love. Even as she is dying, she and Abelard can be lovers in grace; her earthly, physical passion will be purified and transcended by a spiritual union with God who includes all. The dialectic process of Eloisa's renunciation is cogently summarized by Brendan O Hehir:

> Since for Eloisa the struggle between Nature and Grace had been fought out in terms of a choice she was attempting to make between Abelard and Christ, her vision of Abelard as priest presenting to her the Cross of Christ is a revelation that with Christ, both Nature and Grace, Passion and Virtue, are one. Death will effect for her a greater kindness than the quenching of the flames of earthly passion mutilation had effected for Abelard; it will in addition teach her the vanity of all worldly commitments. (311–336) No obstacles remain to the consummation of her marriage to Christ, and that consummation has also, paradoxically, a place for Abelard. But Eloisa no longer looks for a personal reunion in heaven with her earthly lover; the love to be experienced there is diffused and catholic, equally shared by all. When fate shall also have destroyed his fair frame, she prays, "From op'ning skies may streaming glories shine,/ And Saints embrace thee with a love like mine." (341–342)[14]

A little later (343–52) Eloisa envisions herself and Abelard buried in the same tomb, a tomb that will remind future lovers to pity her and Abelard's misfortunes in love. And as these future lovers, at high Mass, "steal a thought from heav'n" to glance from the altar to the tomb, they will be forgiven, since Heaven understands the searing intensity of Eloisa's conflict. Eloisa has attained her vision of Heaven, but she turns earthward; her conflict and its resolution has been too terrible, and it is a last appropriate and "Catholic" gesture of religious devotion to wish that no other lovers suffer the same fate. The end comes in the quiet and full periodic design characteristic of the rich, meditative mnemonic perspective with which she began the poem:

> From the full quire when loud *Hosanna's* rise,
> And swell the pomp of dreadful sacrifice,
> Amid that scene, if some relenting eye
> Glance on the stone where our cold reliques lie,
> Devotion's self shall steal a thought from heav'n,
> One human tear shall drop, and be forgiv'n.
> And sure if fate some future Bard shall join
> In sad similitude of griefs to mine,
> Condemn'd whole years in absence to deplore,
> And image charms he must behold no more,
> Such if there be, who loves so long, so well;
> Let him our sad, our tender story tell;
> The well-sung woes will sooth my pensive ghost;
> He best can paint 'em, who shall feel 'em most.
>
> (353–66)

The "pensive ghost" waiting in purgatory for its final heaven is an appropriate image to end the poem. Her sins will be forgiven: "Ev'n superstition loses ev'ry fear:/ For God, not man, absolves our frailties here." She has bridged the gulf between sense and soul, between earth and Heaven, but only by her death. Tested in an unusual manner, and beyond the capacity of most sinners, she has the right, perhaps, to wish for a poet.

Seldom has the couplet been put to such a difficult use. Eloisa's moments of reminiscence and apparent resignation develop into brief passages of subtle antithetic analysis, which in turn cause sweeps of varied passion that dominate the poem. Within this rhythmic pattern,

Pope fuses couplet structure and design, sentence structure, sound, and diction in a way he did not attempt in
any other major work. The Latin and French types of
compressed inversion in many couplets show his Ovidian
heroine, taut and subtle, in her debate of sense and soul,
suppressing and summarizing emotions that break the
bounds of debate and dialectic in other types of couplets.
The repetition of words and phrases, with a change in
the word or phrase, reflects Eloisa's confusion, her attempt to clarify the "dread" issue that she faces, as well
as her misdirected effort to hold and relive her sensuous
and happier past. Rapid, staccato verbs, nouns, and more
often verb phrases in a series express her flights of passion
as she turns first to Abelard as earthly lover, and then to
him as priest and spiritual lover. Pope mutes the torqued,
recoiling line and half-line characteristic of the *Essay on
Criticism* and *The Rape of the Lock* and with it, the
sharp and brilliant rhyme and pivotal caesura; when the
brilliant balance does occur, it is without Pope's characteristic wit, and more like the Latinate compression and
inversion of Eloisa's controlled meditative and analytical
moments. Pope blends these varied elements of couplet
structure in paragraphs shaped by the rhythm of Eloisa's
conflict, whose violence finds its basic outlet in radical
but brief and sudden contrasts of couplet structure, and
its unity of timbre, color, and mood in Eloisa's rather
formal Latinate language of love and passion, whose syntax and diction owe something to Ovid, to Roman Catholic ritual to Baroque-Metaphysical love poetry, and to
French classical drama. For his passionate nun who uses
a rich and complex past, Pope created a distinctive stylistic decorum; and artist that he was, he used it in this
poem alone.

NOTES

1. Geoffrey Tillotson, Introduction to *Eloisa to Abelard*, *Twick. Ed.*, II, 277–79.

2. *Ibid.*, p. 279.

3. Brendan P. O Hehir, "Virtue and Passion: The Dialectic of *Eloisa to Abelard*," *Texas Studies in Literature and Language*, II (1960), 219–32. This is the best discussion of what Eloisa's conflict of nature and grace is really about, and of the alternatives she is caught between. O Hehir states Eloisa's position clearly, and argues against the position of Henry Pettit, "Pope's *Eloisa to Abelard*: An Interpretation," *University of Colorado Studies, Series in Language and Literature*, No. 4 (Boulder, 1953), pp. 67–74. Pettit sees the poem as employing the pathetic fallacy in its purest form, and argues that Eloisa tries to transcend the division of matter and spirit brought about by Cartesian metaphysics.

4. Tillotson, *op. cit.*, pp. 283–84.

5. *Ibid.*, p. 278

6. *Ibid.*, p. 280.

7. *Twick. Ed.*, II, 298.

8. O Hehir, *op. cit.*, pp. 230–31.

9. This is O Hehir's view and also my own. I have noticed, however, that many students are never convinced that Eloisa has really resolved the conflict; and Brower (*Alexander Pope: The Poetry of Allusion*, p. 81) seems to be less than completely persuaded. He suggests that one is likely to find the poem "remarkable" and "fine," not "moving" or "convincing." O Hehir, pp. 231–32, points out the need for a thorough study and reappraisal of the poem from several aspects.

10. Brower, *op. cit.*, pp. 76, 82–83.

11. *Ibid.*, p. 281.

12. O Hehir interprets "seas of flame" as a naturalistic, physical occurrence; Eloisa is simply blinded by her tears of six lines back (pp. 220–21). While Pettit does not mention this particular line, the implication of his interpretation would make it an instance of the pathetic fallacy. See O Hehir, pp. 219–20.

13. *Op. cit.*, p. 290.

14. *Op. cit.*, pp. 230–31.

7

The Dunciad

THE DUNCIAD VARIORUM 1729

ON A REALISTIC LEVEL the *Dunciad* describes the awakened energies of the world of Dulness, the resultant crowning of an appropriate king, the riotous progress of the dunces through the London streets on their way to invade the polite region of West Minster, and their triumphant progress back to their starting point in the city.[1] The poem pictures the activities of the dunces at the point of gaining control of the literary and cultural world, and as a grand satiric climax, the obliteration of this world when the dunces are victorious. The *Dunciad* is a foreshortened imitation of Virgil's *Aeneid*; and it is the noble and spacious *Aeneid*, always in the background, which helps give form to the poem's rather episodic structure, and which holds it in a mock epic perspective.[2] Important features of Aeneas' removal of his kingdom from Troy to Latium are magnified, but parodied and distorted; the great constructive journey of Prince Aeneas is grotesquely reflected by King Tibbald's ludicrous and ghastly peregrination. But the plot, in itself, is of little interest, nor does Pope's imitation of the *Aeneid* compare with his brilliant parody of epic in *The*

Rape of the Lock. The analogy, however, between the journey of Aeneas to found Rome, and that of Tibbald as he carries the "Smithfield Muses to the ear of Kings" underpins the theme of the work, and is the framework for the more significant action which inheres in the nature of the dunces' activities taken as a whole.

In Book I Pope sets forth the genesis of the goddess Dulness, characterizes Dulness as it manifests itself variously and concretely in London and Grub Street, and describes the Goddess' choice of Tibbald as the new king. In the mock heroic contests of Book II, game after ribald game occurs in rapid succession; in the prophetic Book III, scene after scene of triumphant Dulness is unveiled to Tibbald until the curtain of darkness falls upon the whole mad panorama. Intermittently among all this activity, the goddess Dulness herself, Tibbald, Settle's ghost, and even the lesser dunces assume the stage at various points and act or speak. Since the target of Pope's satire is the contemporary world, the dunces as well as the narrator talk about this world and its history in a concrete fashion. The *Dunciad*, therefore, is densely populated with people and things, and its subject matter is almost encyclopedic in its range. But this great, dense mass of material, articulated in multiple scenes frequently resembling tableaux and skits, is motivated as well as unified by a common theme, which emerges and grows in clarity and power as the motley procession of dunces unfolds: the substitution in the verbal arts of sensationalism, pedantry, and mechanical technique for clarity, strength, and order. The meretricious culture which Pope attacks has been created by dunces who subvert for purposes of their own the classical and Christian ideals of intellect and feeling which together make

up Pope's satiric norm. To mirror the corroding subver-
sion of his norm Pope inverts and parodies not only the
Aeneid, but the Bible, Christian ritual, Milton's *Paradise
Lost,* and lesser works. As a result the poem's range and
variety of allusion and imagery is wider than that of any
other of Pope's poems. But the controlling symbol, the
creating light of intelligence, which is associated with
the *logos* of St. John and Longinus, focuses Pope's dar-
ingly imagined vision of darkening disorder from beginning to end.[3]

Compared with the earlier poems, the texture of the
Dunciad is richer and denser, the action more complex,
and the wit more massive. So Pope created a style that
reflects these differences in several subtle and complex
modifications of his couplet. Clever rhymes, sudden deflations, and brilliant antitheses do occur but are differently designed and are not as sudden and emphatic as in
the earlier poems, for Pope does not depend upon the
antithesis or the incongruous parallel for witty effects.
Before the *Dunciad,* most of Pope's closed couplets are
composed of either two coordinate statements, or of one
sentence whose predicates or objects are compound.
Such a structure makes for a division of the couplet into
neat line or half-line units. This is not to say that there
are not many couplets in the *Dunciad* with neat parallelism and balance, but they are not nearly so frequent as
earlier, and they are subordinated to a different kind of
couplet norm. First, in the *Dunciad,* Pope's techniques
of subordination are more complex and also looser; often
there is more than one subordinate clause in a sentence,
and the clauses are more irregular and fall less neatly into
parallels than earlier. Second, there are many apostrophes, exclamations, and various forms of direct ad-

dress. Third, there are frequent interrupting elements, sudden parentheses and anacoluthon structures. And fourth, the second line is often an ironic appositive of a word in the first line. Instead of balance and laminated parallelism, there is a strategic use of imbalance and enjambment. Syntax and sentence forms are more varied than in earlier poems in order to reflect the narrator's changing satiric focus of his encyclopedic and shifting subject matter. The couplets have a rugged and a direct, proselike structure. The following lines are typical of the majority, and they represent the couplet norm:

> Laborious, heavy, busy, bold, and blind,
> She rul'd in native Anarchy, the mind.
>
> (I. 13–14)

A simple structure, but massive because of the list of weighty, incongruous adjectives and heavy pauses. The second line is awkward because of the displaced "mind" after three unstressed syllables, but like the goddess it describes, it makes a heavy-footed, imbalanced emphasis.

This couplet describes the deficiencies of Tibbald's library, which contains no classics:

> A Gothic Vatican! of Greece and Rome
> Well-purg'd, and worthy Withers, Quarles, and Blome.
>
> (I. 125–26)

The ironic exclamation creates a strong pause. Then the swift, run-on unit stops suddenly, quickly followed by the list of dunces, which makes two more pauses. Pope works an alliterative pun: "worthy" modifies in two directions; it describes "Vatican," and because "of" is omitted, ironically calls the dunces "worthy."

Here is another example of a structure that occurs
more frequently in the *Duncaid* than perhaps in any
other of Pope's poems:

> Inspir'd he seizes: These an altar raise:
> An hecatomb of pure, unsully'd lays. . . .
>
> (I. 137–38)

This couplet does not look like one that would be found
in a previous work; except for the rhyme it hardly looks
like a couplet at all. But one does not read couplets in
isolation, and here is the matrix passage:

> Of these twelve volumes, twelve of amplest size,
> Redeem'd from tapers and defrauded pyres,
> Inspir'd he seizes: These an altar raise:
> An hecatomb of pure, unsully'd lays
> That altar crowns: A folio Common-place
> Founds the whole pyle, of all his works the base;
> Quarto's, Octavo's, shape the less'ning pyre,
> And last, a little Ajax tips the spire.   (I. 135–42)

The lines are incomplete to the last couplet, and the
structure is indirect and periodic, exaggerating the piling
of the books in a mock epic manner. Then the last
couplet ends with the appropriate directness and neat-
ness as the "little Ajax" is put carefully atop the pyr-
amid. The passage moves from a rough, irregular, imbalanced design to the contrasting design of the last couplet
without any sense of stylistic incongruity.

The next example,

> With that she gave him (piteous of his case,
> Yet smiling at his rueful length of face),
>
> (II. 133–34)

is simply another instance of the lack of neatly designed parallelism in the *Dunciad*, and of the interrupting, anacoluthon modifier. The satirist starts a sentence, but must tell the reader the whole truth by inserting some sort of ironic qualification between the main elements of the beginning and end of the sentence.

In the following the first rhyme word suggests an indecent ambiguity which in the second line is capped by a satirical appositive of the meaning of the whole first line:

> So swells each Windpipe; Ass intones to Ass,
> Harmonic twang! of leather, horn, and brass.
> (II. 243–44)

The couplet has powers other than its ambiguity. The first line is slightly iambic; all the syllables receive about the same emphasis, creating the sense of effort denoted by the statement. The second line is strictly iambic, and the thumping iambs of the objects of prepositions in fact make the harmonious twang appropriate for the sonic abusiveness of the couplet.

The next couplet, like the one above, illustrates the sound quality that Pope employs so often with satiric effect, and also the rugged directness of the norm couplets:

> Some strain in rhyme; the Muses, on their racks,
> Scream, like the winding of ten thousand Jacks.
> (III. 153–54)

The run-on structure of the couplet is disguised by the addition of the prepositional phrase in the first line, "on their racks," while the completing verb, "Scream," comes in the emphatic first position. The placement of "on

their racks" enables Pope to get a harsh interplay of
cracking rhymes and whining nasals. Even if one has
never heard the screeching of an old-fashioned, wooden
jackscrew, he can understand the sound quality Pope was
trying to achieve here, and can even afford to overlook
the two scatological puns.

Sometimes Pope will put an awkward, limping,
three-unit line against a two-unit one, so that we get
three pauses against two, as in this passage where the
subject of the couplet is a copious author of law books
and a heavy-handed literary critic to boot:

> Jacob, the Scourge of Grammar, mark with awe,
> Nor less revere him, Blunderbuss of Law.
>   (III. 149–50)

The division of the second line, which forces an awkward
pause in the middle of the third foot, is as ungainly as
the heavy collocation of consonants in the middle of the
first line and in the second half of the last. The sound
and movement characterize the victim—heavy, ugly,
clumsy.

These examples of isolated couplets barely skim the
surface of Pope's variety. But one can see that they are
more boldly structured than those of the earlier poems,
more rugged, and that the inversions are less neatly patterned. The dynamics of Pope's couplet becomes clearer,
however, when we look at how he masses his couplets, an
arresting feature of the *Dunciad's* satiric art. Five of the
seven examples above are closed couplets, and they resemble more closely the open couplets of the poem than
is typical of earlier poems where passages of open couplets are often contrasted with closed couplets. The same
degree of contrast is not characteristic of the *Duncaid;*

for while it contains distinctively designed passages which are unlike the norm, the couplet norm is more closely interwoven in these passages and throughout the poem than is typical of Pope up to 1728.

This is the opening invocation:

> Books and the Man I sing, the first who brings
> 2 The Smithfield Muses to the Ear of Kings.
> Say great Patricians! (since your selves inspire
> 4 These wond'rous works; so Jove and Fate require)
> Say from what cause, in vain descry'd and curst,
> 6 Still Dunce the second reigns like Dunce the first?
> In eldest time, e'er mortals writ or read,
> 8 E'er Pallas issued from the Thund'rer's head,
> Dulnes o'er all possess'd her antient right,
> 10 Daughter of Chaos and eternal Night:
> Fate in their dotage this fair idiot gave,
> 12 Gross as her sire, and as her mother grave,
> Laborious, heavy, busy, bold, and blind,
> 14 She rul'd, in native Anarchy, the mind.   (I. 1–14)

Several things set this apart from Pope's earlier styles. The first couplet is closed and then follow three sentences, each composed of two couplets. Balance is absent and the parallelism is neutral. The forward movement by balance and recoil as in the *Essay on Criticism* and *The Rape of the Lock* is gone. Although the twelfth line is a chiasmus, the first half points backward to the preceding line, and the second half forward to the next line; the neat syntax of the usual chiasmus which collapses inward upon the point of division is missing. The last couplet is a run-on structure of the preceding one, very different from the pointed closure in the early works. There are few adjectives compared with the early poems, and each is necessary and functional, an integral part of its noun rather than a modifier. Except for the use of more enjambment and longer subordinations, these couplets suggest the masterful contempt of Dryden's "mighty line." Appropriately Dulness is given, if one may say so, an absurd but portentous majesty.

Even the anaphoral parallelism of the *Dunciad* is more open and suspended, more varied and complex than earlier:

> Here to her Chosen all her works she shows;
> 2 Prose swelled to verse, Verse loitring into prose;
> How random Thoughts now meaning chance to find,
> 4 Now leave all memory of sense behind:
> How Prologues into Prefaces decay,
> 6 And these to Notes are fritter'd quite away.
> How Index-learning turns no student pale,
> 8 Yet holds the Eel of science by the Tail.
> How, with less reading than makes felons 'scape,
> 10 Less human genius than God gives an ape,
> Small thanks to France, and none to Rome or Greece,
> 12 A past, vamp'd, future, old, reviv'd, new piece,
> 'Twixt Plautus, Fletcher, Congreve, and Corneille,
> 14 Can make a Cibber, Johnson, or Ozell.   (I. 227–40)

The first eight lines are not unusual, but none are divided except the second whose chiasmus is achieved without syntactic inversion. The concluding six lines, a kind of sestet, gather up and apply the concretes of the octet. Pope uses a simple grammar and syntax in the controlling lines but inserts complicating modifying lines, then throws the lines into sudden, destructive completion with the jab of the last line predicate. Bolder and freer than usual, Pope is willing to risk more; the balance is gone and along with it the over-careful grammar of his earlier anaphoral designs. These are not the couplets of much of the *Pastorals*, *Windsor-Forest*, or the *Essay on Criticism*, but a vehement, pell-mell oration with the overlapping repetition characteristic of speech rather than writing.

Book II describes the heroic games in which the dunces vie with one another for the favor of their goddess by engaging in all kinds of absurd, nonsensical activities; and if the descriptions are sometimes filthy and scatological, they represent the ugliness of bad culture and the monstrous, deforming powers of the mind of Dulness. The opening of Book II is a heroic burlesque of Milton's description of the throne of Satan:

> High on a gorgeous seat, that far outshone
> Henley's gilt Tub, or Fleckno's Irish Throne,
> Or that, where on her Curlls the Public pours
> All-bounteous, fragrant grains, and golden show'rs;
> Great Tibbald sate: the Proud Parnassian sneer,
> The conscious simper, and the jealous leer,
> Mix on his look. All eyes direct their rays
> On him, and crowds grow foolish as they gaze.
>
> (II. 1–8)

The brazen foolishness of the meaning is set off by the mighty dignity of the style. In the space of just four couplets Pope employs three run-on lines and a possible fourth one if the predicate, "Mix on his look," is read as a run-on. The open, run-on couplets with their odd sounds create a ludicrous Miltonic majesty out of the Popean couplet. The oddly fused components call attention to one another, but the tightly related rhymes easily fuse with the blank verse quality to underscore the vulgar serenity of Tibbald's coronation.

The coronation sets the stage for the heroic games. In the couplets describing these, Pope often uses run-on

lines to create ironic disparities between means and ends,
and between structure and meaning and sound. His use
of particular sound patterns is organic to the satire, but
just as effective, however, is the couplet structure and
design, the form which molds it. In the next example a
run-on is joined with balanced hemistichs to bring off a
humorous effect. Dulness proposes a urinary contest:

> The Goddess then: 'Who best can send on high
> The salient spout, far-streaming to the sky;
> His be yon Juno of majestic size,
> With cow-like–udders, and ox-like eyes.'
>
> (II. 153–56)

The run-on structure and thunderous diction of the first
couplet is deflated, or perhaps inflated, by the details
the last line in metronomic, sing-song parallels.

Later when Curl and Osborne accept the challenge,
Pope contrasts their efforts. Osborne is contending:

> A second effort brought but new disgrace,
> For straining more, it flies in his own face;
> Thus the small jett which hasty hands unlock,
> Squirts in the gard'ner's eyes who turns the cock.
> Not so from shameless Curl: Impetuous spread
> The stream, and smoking, flourish'd o'er his head.
>
> (II. 167–72)

The end-topped lines give way to Curl's triumph; and
not only does the last couplet impetuously proclaim vic-
tory, but it does so in a form suddenly appropriate, for
the run-on line reflects the power and swiftness of
Curl's stream.

When a sentence concludes in the middle of a line it
frequently prepares for a surprise. Here Dulness exhorts

her dunces to learn well the power of noise, noise without form and meaning:

> 'Now turn to diff'rent sports (the Goddess cries)
> 2 And learn, my sons, the wond'rous pow'r of Noise.
> To move, to raise, to ravish ev'ry heart,
> 4 With Shakespeare's nature, or with Johnson's art,
> Let others aim: 'Tis yours to shake the soul
> 6 With thunder rumbling from the mustard-bowl.'
>
> (II. 213–18)

After the ambiguous injunction to learn the power of noise, the periodic structure starts building its edifice in the second couplet by repeating an honored truism about two great writers. The context of rebellion against good writing must be made clear, for Dulness wants no part of Shakespeare and Jonson, so the brief clause at the beginning of line 5, "Let others aim," reverses the expectation aroused by the first part of the sentence and sets the stage for the final, heroic run-on sentence which collapses the edifice. In true duncely fashion, the climax comes in the thunder machine with which dunces delight idiots. The satirical reversal, one should note, is achieved by an irregular antithesis that takes up four lines in norm couplets, very different from the neatly balanced antithesis of the early poems. This type of design, typical of the satire in the *Dunciad*, is a fine example of Pope's own "art of sinking in poetry."

The examples cited thus far are not meant to give the impression that all the couplets of the *Dunciad* are rougher and more constantly varied in structure, more imbalanced than in Pope's earlier poems. They are not, of course; but even in a passage whose syntax is straight and simple, there is usually a structural quality present

that is distinctive of the *Dunciad* alone. In the marvelous parodic adaptation that follows, Tibbald, like Aeneas
in the sixth book of the *Aeneid,* has descended to the
Elysian shades to see the souls of unborn mortals preparing for birth and return to the world. These souls are
nothing but the literary creations of dunces struggling to
get published and flood the land:

> And now, on Fancy's easy wing convey'd,
> 2 The King descended to th' Elyzian shade.
> There, in a dusky vale where Lethe rolls,
> 4 Old Bavius sits, to dip poetic souls,
> And blunt the sense, and fit it for a scull
> 6 Of solid proof, impenetrably dull.
> Instant when dipt, away they wing their flight,
> 8 Where Brown and Mears unbar the gates of Light,
> Demand new bodies, and in Calf's array
> 10 Rush to the world, impatient for the day.
> Millions and millions on these banks he views,
> 12 Thick as the stars of night, or morning dews,
> As thick as bees o'er vernal blossoms fly,
> 14 As thick as eggs at Ward in Pillory.   (III. 13–26)

Neutral parallels carry a grotesquerie resembling the
half-ugly Alice-in-Wonderland effect of the Cave of
Spleen passage in *The Rape of the Lock*. Here are the
gates of an inverted paradise. The rich, smooth diction
which alludes to Virgilian mythology and which employs
such hackneyed poeticisms as "Fancy's easy wing,"
"dusky vale," "morning dews," and "vernal blossoms," is
carried by a simple, rapid syntax which throws the allusions into juxtaposition with other, not-so-pretty terms.
The second and third couplets (3–6) march smoothly
along with a straightforward ordering of the sentence

parts. This smoothness emphasizes the short *i* sounds as well as the popping, ticking, stopped consonants, especially when they are climaxed by the difficult sounds of "impenetrably"; then the sibilants and stopped consonants of the whole couplet suddenly ease away into "dull." The next sentence (7–10) is swift and direct. "Rush," in the first position, emphasizes its speed, but "Calf's array" is incongruous, as are the flat, common names of the booksellers Brown and Mears who perform an inappropriately beautiful and mythic action. The anaphoral parallels of the last three lines repeat "thick," a kind of pun for "stupid," and with their tritely splendid diction suddenly run into a line filled with ugly content whose harsh, flat "eggs at Ward in Pillory" throws the whole passage into an ugly and disreputable perspective.

Pope has literally sung about a noble and poetic classical myth in this rapid, flowing passage, combining the beautiful and the absurd without a break. And, as in the best art, the ugly and ridiculous is emphasized by a splendid and shapely passage. The "objective" facts of the situation as Pope names and describes them accomplish the satiric effect without any of the techniques turning upon balance used in the *Essay on Criticism* and *The Rape of the Lock*. Incomplete norm couplets in 5–6 and 9–10 and the directness of the whole give the passage a ruggedness and simplicity which characterizes the narrator and enables him to use "beautiful" allusions and poetic diction with scathing sarcastic directness.

The last example, which follows below, illustrates again Pope's rich satire, and also his strategic reluctance in the *Dunciad* to smash his target with a single sharp blow. Settle's ghost, Tibbald's guide to the mock under-

world, has shown Tibbald the vulgar wonders of the
eighteenth century stage, then he singles out a particular
genius:

> 'Son! what thou seek'st is in thee. Look and find
> 2 Each monster meets his likeness in thy mind.
> Yet would'st thou more? In yonder cloud, behold!
> 4 Whose sarcenet skirts are edg'd with flamy gold,
> A matchless youth: His nod these worlds controuls,
> 6 Wings the red lightning, and the thunder rolls.
> Angel of Dulness, sent to scatter round
> 8 Her magic charms o'er all unclassic ground:
> Yon stars, yon suns, he rears at pleasure higher,
> 10 Illumes their light, and sets their flames on fire.
> Immortal Rich! how calm he sits at ease
> 12 Mid snows of paper, and fierce hail of pease;
> And proud his mistress' orders to perform,
> 14 Rides in the whirlwind, and directs the storm.
>   (III. 247–60)

This easy, eloquent satire has a structural rhythm all its
own. It goes from "monster," a burlesque Platonic archetype in the mind of Dulness and all her sons, to the
"matchless youth," then shifts to a satiric appositive,
"Angel of Dulness," with his divine mission. Then, with
the soaring parallels, to the specific target, to the name of
the man himself—"Immortal Rich." Next his Angelic
mission is satirically brought to ground as we see him
suddenly as only a clever mechanic of the theatre, making lightning, snow, and storms with fireworks, paper,
and peas. But away he flies again like God himself who
rides the whirlwind and directs the storm. The strength
of this passage is first of all dependent on the context of
the monstrous and absurd in theatrical productions; yet
Pope succeeds in making vulgarity and tawdriness expres-

sive by passing from the direct and colloquial (1–2), to inflated, rhetorical inversion (3–5), to the straightforward rolling parallelism of the other lines which suggests Zeus in his chariot, and ironically God of the Psalms. Can one fail to substitute for Rich any number of famous Hollywood producers?

All of the passages we have examined, whether composed of a majority of open or closed couplets, fall within the description of the couplet norm. One would assume this; but in some of Pope's poems, notably *The Rape of the Lock*, the couplet norm is more sharply differentiated from the particular designs of many passages. This is not the case in the *Dunciad* where the norm couplets occur more constantly throughout the poem than is characteristic of Pope in the earlier works with the possible exception of *Eloisa to Abelard*. Nor are couplets of similar structures—that is, couplets in balances or parallels, noun clusters, absolute constructions, or other structures—bound together in unified passages in order to express a particular theme or motif to the same extent as earlier. They are dispersed throughout the poem but are consistently dominated by the couplet norm. The brilliant parody, the sarcastic mockery, the passages which imitate or represent a characteristic of a victim, an idea, or a situation, are held in stylistic perspective by the norm which expresses finally the constant and deeper attitude of the Satirist toward his subject and theme. Dulness—no matter how comic, ugly, or silly its particular manifestations—is, after all, a mighty and honored adversary. The values the Satirist defends are crucially significant, and their peril is great. The Satirist's attitude, behind all his particular attacks, must be touched with sullen dignity and sweeping disdain. As a result, the asymmetrical, imbalanced, and complicated couplets of the *Dunciad's* norm embody a rugged and powerful utterance, which was carried to an even fuller fruition in the *Dunciad* of 1743, especially by the majestic sweep of its fourth book.

THE DUNCIAD OF 1743

When Pope published the new *Dunciad* in 1743, with Cibber instead of Theobald as hero, he added the long fourth book, rewrote the previous three books of the *Dunciad Variorum* of 1729, and with some changes, shifted the earlier ending of Book III to the end of Book IV, the famous ending in which many think Pope wrote his noblest poetry. We must not forget, however, that the ending of the 1743 version is a revised version of the 1729 ending, and stylistically they are almost alike.[4] Pope made many small alterations in the first three books, rewriting some sections, omitting some, and adding short sections and individual couplets here and there. Mainly, however, the couplet styles of the two versions are closely similar, and Book IV effortlessly continues the style of 1729. The differences are matters of refinement of structure and nuance depending on small changes in sound and rhythm, and more frequently on a reshaping or refocusing of meaning. A discussion of the *Dunciad* of 1743, and particularly of its added fourth book, therefore, is put at this point in Pope's career to show that the couplet style of the 1743 version is essentially the same as that of the 1729 version, and to avoid the inconvenience of treating the *Dunciad* in two widely separated chapters.

Pope's style is slightly bolder and more massive than

in the earlier version. For example, the designs of the opening are similar, but that of the Variorum suffers a little when compared with the more sweeping invocation of the later poem. Here are the two openings, the Variorum first:

> Books and the Man I sing, the first who brings
> The Smithfield Muses to the Ear of Kings.
> Say great Patricians! (since your selves inspire
> These wond'rous works; so Jove and Fate require)
> Say from what cause, in vain descry'd and curst
> Still Dunce the second reigns like Dunce the first?
>
> (I. 1–6)

And now the later opening:

> The Mighty Mother, and her Son who brings
> The Smithfield Muses to the ear of Kings,
> I sing. Say you, her instruments the Great!
> Call'd to this work by Dulness, Jove, and Fate;
> You by whose care, in vain descry'd and curst,
> Still Dunce the second reigns like Dunce the first;
> Say how the Goddess bade Britannia sleep,
> And pour'd her Spirit o'er the land and deep.
>
> (I. 1–8)

The opening sentence of the second version is more forceful and sustained. Sonorous, inverted, and run-on, it is suddenly thrown into completion with the sullen plunge of "I sing," which summarizes more and promises more than it does in the neater but less emphatic placing of the first version. The parallels of the second opening are also more sustained; and the addition of the fourth couplet with the connecting repetition of "Say" rolls out and expands the meaning beyond the first opening.

To show further this added sweep of sullen eloquence, here is the opening of Book IV:

>   Yet, yet a moment, one dim Ray of Light
> 2 Indulge, dread Chaos, and eternal Night!
>   Of darkness visible so much be lent,
> 4 As half to shew, half veil the deep Intent.
>   Ye Pow'rs! whose Mysteries restor'd I sing,
> 6 To whom Time bears me on his rapid wing,
>   Suspend a while your Force inertly strong,
> 8 Then take at once the Poet and the Song.
>   (IV. 1–8)

Slow and intense, the first couplet introduces the portentous theme of final darkness. Its inversion puts the emphasis on Chaos and Night, whose literal meaning is obvious, for Pope begs them to wait; and "eternal Night" is simply the mode of direct address. But the couplet as well as the passage suggest that eternal Night is approaching inexorably, about to overwhelm the poet while he raises his hand to stay it briefly. The Miltonic inversion of the second couplet, also closed, emphasizes the parallels of line 4. Lifting his voice again, the poet addresses the powers to make the same point but with a different emphasis. To drive home the urgency, Pope concludes with a verse of four lines, each line of which, remaining incomplete, takes the thought in four different directions. First the subject, "Pow'rs," then two dimensions, "whose" and "to whom," and last the compound verbs which throw "Pow'rs" into final action, "suspend" and "take." The particulars of the passage are focused by the following design: two short movements of one couplet each give way to a longer movement which intensifies the meaning by holding up the inexorable arrival of Chaos and Night who will immolate the creator of the vision, the poet himself. With a rising effort to stay the destruction awaiting him, he ends with the magnificent gesture of the final line, inviting the mighty forces to hurl him into the abyss. A new and powerful note is struck, for the Satirist realizes in a perilous sense his deep involvement with the mighty forces he is singing.

More than any other of Pope's satires, the *Dunciad* expresses toward its victims a serene and almost lyrical contempt. The professors of Oxford and Cambridge who still reject Locke because he is radically different from Aristotle, and Dr. Richard Bentley, the Aristarchus of the poem, are the victims in the next passage; but the masterful verse transcends Bentley as Pope's personal victim, and we leave it with a sense only of Pope's satiric creativity:

> Prompt at the call, around the Goddess roll
> 2 Broad hats, and hoods, and caps, a sable shoal:
> Thick and more thick the black blockade extends,
> 4 A hundred head of Aristotle's friends.
> Nor wert thou, Isis! wanting to the day,
> 6 [Tho' Christ-church long kept prudishly away.]
> Each staunch Polemic, stubborn as a rock,
> 8 Each fierce Logician, still expelling Locke,
> Came whip and spur, and dash'd thro' thin and thick
> 10 On German Crousaz, and Dutch Burgersdyck.
> As many quit the streams that murm'ring fall
> 12 To lull the sons of Marg'ret and Clare-hall,
> Where Bentley late tempestuous wont to sport
> 14 In troubled waters, but now sleeps in Port.
>
> (IV. 189–202)

The first couplet presents the agitated frumpery of an academic procession revolving in disordered solicitation

around Dulness, its natural center of "gravity." "Roll"
enjambs the line, and "hats," "hoods," and "caps," in
clipped iambic meter give the line a flippant, smacking
quality. The guttural stops of line 3 make the line thick
and heavy, but fittingly, for the members of the "black
blockade" are numbered in the next line like so many
head of cattle. At the fourth couplet (7–8) the subject of
each line, "Polemic" and "Logician," is sharply modified
and armed by the second half of each line: "stubborn as
a rock," and "still expelling Locke." In line 9 they suddenly come through, "whip and spur," after the two
half–line modifiers hold them off. The two victims,
whose names are full of hissing sibilants and harsh consonants, tend to burst apart the neatly balanced line. "Ger-
man Crousaz" and "Dutch Burgersdyck" are presumably
on the Satirist's side since they defend Locke, but the
content and movement of the lines, as well as their
sounds, reduce the epic–academic contest to triviality.
Then in line 11 the sound changes, the tone softens, and
the design grows swifter, smoother, and neutral without
the hammered appositives and half-line qualifications of
the first five couplets. Like the flowing of a stream, it
mock-poetically and softly rolls Bentley into "Port," and
into a pun (wine). The special élan of this passage lies in
its combination of different couplet structures, its
rhythms and tone colors. As in *The Rape of the Lock*,
here is apt and suggestive language, wit and grace, but
Pope's couplet norm working throughout the passage
gives these lines a strength and ruggedness characteristic
of the *Dunciad* alone.

The bewildering variety of designs in the 1743 version
makes representative selection difficult, although the
couplet norm is evident everywhere. Whatever kind of

passage one wishes to find is in the poem. I choose the following longer one because it represents Pope's genius for satiric mimicry, and because I know of no passage that quite performs the function of this one. Late in Book IV the virtuoso-naturalists crowd around the goddess Dulness to testify to their accomplishments and to give her a votive offering:

> Then thick as Locusts black'ning all the ground,
> A tribe, with weeds and shells fantastic crown'd,
> Each with some wond'rous gift approach'd the Pow'r,
> A Nest, a Toad, a Fungus, or a Flow'r.   (IV. 397–400)

In the first couplet Pope nicely dispenses with explicit grammar; the tribe seems to suddenly appear without the aid of a narrator. The second couplet, too, has a graphic compression, and the reader's attention is thrown upon the four nouns which make the satiric point by simply being there.[5]

The "virtuoso" with the flower makes his speech explaining how he previously cultivated it, and then accuses a rival of destroying his flower by capturing a butterfly that alighted on it:

> 'And lo the wretch! whose vile, whose insect lust,
> Lay'd this gay daughter of the Spring in dust.
> Oh punish him, or to th' Elysian shades
> Dismiss my soul, where no Carnation fades!'
>   (IV. 415–18)

The accused answers in a speech similar to the harangue of his accuser:

> 'Of all th' enamel'd race, whose silv'ry wing
> 2 Waves to the tepid Zephyrs of the spring,

Or swims along the fluid atmosphere,
4 Once brightest shin'd this child of Heat and Air.
I saw, and started from its vernal bow'r
6 The rising game, and chac'd from flow'r to flow'r.
It fled, I follow'd; now in hope, now pain;
8 It stopt, I stopt; it mov'd, I mov'd again.
At last it fix'd, 'twas on what plant it pleas'd,
10 And where it fix'd, the beauteous bird I seiz'd:
Rose or Carnation was below my care;
12 I meddle, Goddess! only in my sphere.
I tell the naked fact without disguise,
14 And, to excuse it, need but shew the prize;
Whose spoils this paper offers to your eye,
16 Fair ev'n in death! this peerless *Butterfly*.'
(IV. 421–36)

The generalized description of the butterfly is not striking, except perhaps in its perfect sense of decorum; but
the movement of this "enamelled" diction, as its periodic form builds up to "child of Heat and Air," catches
the butterfly's essence. In the next three couplets
(5–10), Pope describes the chase in lines unusual in
their number of pauses, and in their mincing,
over-careful repetition. This effeminate, exacting quality
of the short clauses expresses the character of the actor
who compulsively describes every movement of the in-
consequential pursuit. At last the final couplets grow
more neutrally structured, the actor grows more abstract,
and with the subordination and inversion of the final
two couplets, comes to an overwhelming climax. Appropriately the butterfly is not named until the final words;
and although we knew what it is, it comes as a slight
shock after such a beautiful to-do to hear it flatly named.
The quality of the diction and the peculiar movement of
the lines create a hothouse picture of beautified death

which suggests the dessicated, asexual quality of the naturalist whose soul is bounded in the glittering corpse of the butterfly. Pope's contempt allows the naturalist to shrivel himself into an image of his trophy.

Such imitation or mimicry occurs under many guises in either *Dunciad*. There is so much of it in Book IV, and so many distinctive and expressive passages about a variety of duncely activities, that Pope's satiric virtuosity blinds many readers to his developing theme. At the end, however, all the complexities of the poem are suddenly generalized, and fused, by the blazing coda. The ending is a burlesque celebration of the powers of the word; but the import of the preceding satire is so heightened and intensified by the infernal majesty of Pope's vision that the conclusion is lyric. First, however, let us take the ending of Book III of 1729, then compare it with the ending of Book IV in order to see how Pope improved the later ending. Here is the earlier conclusion:

> 'Signs following signs lead on the Mighty Year;
> See! the dull stars roll round and re-appear.
> She comes! the Cloud-compelling Pow'r, behold!
> With Night Primaeval, and with Chaos old.
> Lo! the great Anarch's ancient reign restor'd,
> Light dies before her uncreating word:
> As one by one, at dread Medaea's strain,
> The sick'ning Stars fade off th' aethereal plain;
> As Argus' eyes, by Hermes' wand opprest,
> Clos'd one by one to everlasting rest:
> Thus at her felt approach, and secret might,
> Art after Art goes out, and all is Night.
> See sculking Truth in her old cavern lye,
> Secur'd by mountains of heap'd casuistry:
> Philosophy that touch'd the Heavens before,
> Shrinks to her hidden cause, and is no more:
> See Physic beg the Stagyrite's defence!

See Metaphysic call for aid on Sence!
See Mystery to Mathematicks fly!
In vain! they gaze, turn giddy, rave, and die.
Thy hand great Dulness! lets the curtain fall,
And universal Darkness covers all.'
   'Enough! enough!' the raptur'd Monarch cries;
And thro' the Ivory Gate the Vision flies.

                                          (III. 335–58)

Pope must have thought this passage so good that he
could think only of a modification as the proper conclusion for the fourth book in 1743. In the first conclusion
the progression of growing darkness begins with the uncreating word of Dulness, and then goes from the arts to
truth, to philosophy, to medicine, to metaphysics and
mathematics. At this point, let us look at the conclusion
of Book IV:

       In vain, in vain,—the all-composing Hour
2 Resistless falls: The Muse obeys the Pow'r.
   She comes! she comes! the sable Throne behold
4 Of *Night* Primaeval, and of *Chaos* old!
   Before her, *Fancy's* gilded clouds decay,
6 And all its varying Rain-bows die away.
   Wit shoots in vain its momentary fires,
8 The meteor drops, and in a flash expires.
   As one by one, at dread Medea's strain,
10 The sick'ning stars fade off th' ethereal plain;
   As Argus' eyes by Hermes' wand opprest,
12 Clos'd one by one to everlasting rest;
   Thus at her felt approach and secret might,
14 *Art* after *Art* goes out, and all is Night,
   See skulking *Truth* to her old Cavern fled,
16 Mountains of Casuistry heap'd o'er her head!
   Philosophy, that lean'd on Heav'n before,
18 Shrinks to her second cause, and is no more.
   Physic of *Metaphysic* begs defence,

20 And *Metaphysic* calls for aid on Sense!
   See Mystery to Mathematics fly!
22 In vain! they gaze, turn giddy, rave, and die.
   Religion blushing veils her sacred fires,
24 And unawares *Morality* expires.
   Nor *public* Flame, nor *private*, dares to shine;
26 Nor *human* Spark is left, nor glimpse *divine!*
   Lo! thy dread Empire, CHAOS! is restor'd;
28 Light dies before thy uncreating word:
   Thy hand, great Anarch! lets the curtain fall;
30 And Universal Darkness buries All.   (IV. 627–56)

As Dulness falls upon the whole nation, she also envelops the Satirist's muse who falls asleep and can tell him no more (619–26). Then the order of dying is similar to that of the first conclusion, except that this time darkness sweeps on to religion and to public and private virtue. Then the last spark and divine glimpse die away, obliterated by the curtain of dulness which hides from men their relations to a divinely ordered universe, and which analogously perverts and deforms the powers of language to create, to order, and to clarify. The progression of the later ending is a greater and more comprehensive movement than the earlier one. Brooks and Wimsatt call the conclusion "sublimely chaotic" and "profoundly dark."[6] Aubrey Williams notes cogently the reason for the climactic putting out of the light:

The concluding events of the poem are a progression of images in a phantasmagoric movement by which Pope reveals the powers of duncery at their supreme and final work of bathetic unfulfilment, at their climactic task of negation. For surely the poet in the conclusion of his poem is engaged in a new counterpoise of Longinian sublime and Cibberian profound. In opposition to the sublimity and magnificence attributed by Longinus to

the divine command, 'Let there be light,' he has involved the duncers in the greatest act of bathos, their
deity's command of 'Let there be darkness.'[7]

The command is achieved. Utterly and completely
this is the end, and there is no need for creating in the
verse a sense of further continuity. So overpowering is
the spectacle that Pope's overt forms of wit and irony are
put away. They are out of place now, since even he as
Satirist is overwhelmed by a deity whose "uncreating
word" makes the night of the mind. He can do nothing
but describe the engulfing of his world and there is
nothing more to say. But the irony of the final situation
turns upon the Satirist to involve him with his audience
in a significant way. Throughout the poem Pope has
satirized dunces and the powers of Dulness with a variety
of brilliant techniques, and in Book IV, which is an
organic summation of the whole, has ironically sung the
overrunning of an ordered, divinely oriented civilization
by the blind, deforming forces of Dulness embodied in
the archetypal rule of a primordial goddess of chaos. But
with great insight, Pope all along has made the goddess
represent a quality which infuses all men and which they
share with nonhuman nature as well: the tendency to
obey gravity, to fall to chaos unless sustained by a higher
power. In the poem, Dulness is always associated with
heaviness and vagueness, with intellectual and artistic
apathy, with the unthinking "comfort" of the "uncreating word." In many ways it is easier and pleasanter to be
a dunce than to follow the cultural and literary ideal
implied throughout the poem. So Dulness finally is a
sinister and dangerous force; it does have a grotesque
sublimity, and Pope rises to his subject with a fierce sense

of creativity and with a controlled but deeply charged lyricism.

For all these reasons, then, the satiric and ironic indirection of the whole poem is suddenly straightened out and climaxed by the direct, uncomplicated conclusion. The force and intensity of the Satirist's statement of what he sees is the main thing; and the structural "secrets" can be quickly divulged. There are few inversions, even those common to Pope's couplet. The passage moves fast until the two closing couplets where it is slowed almost to a stop by the tension between its metrics and the urgency of its meaning and tone. Pope strains the iambic norm to its limits. In the final four lines, each monosyllabic word, except the two articles, requires more emphasis than it "iambically" deserves. All the lines, especially the last four, are spare, and the more complicated sentence patterns of most of the poem are missing. Except in lines 9–12, one straightforward, linear, declarative statement follows another to carry the darkly beautiful imagery and to emphasize the verbs of sinking, falling and dying; and each sentence creates a mounting significance until the climax comes in the last two intense, majestic couplets.

What was said of the couplet style of the earlier *Dunciad* is true of the later one, except with this difference: the fourth book shows stylistically perfect ease in rapid shifts of couplet style and modes of rhetoric, and in complicated satiric description embodied more constantly in the couplet norm. The writing of the *Essay on Man*, the *Moral Essays*, and the *Imitations of Horace* during the 1730's had made Pope a more consummate artist with the couplet—if such a thing is possible—than he was earlier; certainly his couplets reflect the structural patterns and even the sounds of speech with more ease and variety than in the *Dunciad Variorum*. So except for these slight refinements, except for greater smoothness and economy in open passages, and more varied structures without balance, Pope could well have written the couplets of the 1743 *Dunciad* in 1729. When one considers what Pope wrote between the two main versions of the poem, the similarity of couplet styles is surprising. He leaped back over his styles of fourteen years and picked up the style of 1729 without a break. The main difference is that he learned how to give complex material a more urgent and personal tone by deepening and universalizing his theme. The Satirist became more profoundly involved with his theme, and so does the reader.

NOTES

1. The itinerary of the dunces is clearly described, and with a rich sense of its significance, by Aubrey L. Williams, *Pope's Dunciad: A Study of Its Meaning* (London: Methuen and Co. Ltd., 1955), pp. 29–41.

2. See Williams' discussion of Pope's use of the *Aeneid. Ibid.*, pp. 16–29.

3. Thomas R. Edwards, Jr., "Light and Nature: A Reading of the *Dunciad*," *Philological Quarterly*, XXXIX (Oct. 1960), 447–63. Also, *This Dark Estate: A Reading of Pope* (Berkeley and Los Angeles: University of California Press, 1963), pp. 116–30. See also, Williams, pp. 131–56.

4. See *Twick. Ed.* V, 2nd ed. (1953), ed. James Sutherland, for the texts of the two poems; and the one volume edition of the Twickenham text, ed. John Butt, New Haven: Yale University Press, 1963.

5. F. R. Leavis notes the last line of this passage as symbolizing the "packed heterogeneity" of the *Dunciad*, and as an example of Pope's creative delight in the "rich strangeness" and "varied absurdities of the human scene." *The Common Pursuit* (London: Penguin Books, 1963), pp. 94–95.

6. *Literary Criticism: A Short History* (New York: Alfred A. Knopf, 1957), p. 246. The passage is significant: "The revised Fourth Book of the *Dunciad*, especially in its sublimely chaotic and profoundly dark conclusion, is a burlesque celebration of the 'word,' so radical, so metaphysical, Platonic, and Patristic, that it goes far to return the neoclassic argument to a place in its history where it connects with the remote sources of Vichian and romantic symbolism."

7. *Op. cit.*, p. 154.

8

ꙮ

Moral Essays: *Epistle IV*
To Richard Boyle, Earl of Burlington
1731

AFTER THE *Dunciad Variorum* in 1729, Pope published
next the *Epistle to Richard Boyle, Earl of Burlington* in
1731, which appeared in the Warburton edition of 1751
as *Moral Essay IV*. At the same time that Pope was
writing the *Epistle to Burlington*, he was apparently
working on the *Epistle to Allen Lord Bathurst*, not published until 1733. From 1730 to 1733 he was writing the
Essay on Man, published during 1733 and 1734.[1] Thus,
aside from the fact that it is a major work, there are good
chronological reasons for considering the *Essay on Man*
next in this study. I omit the *Essay on Man*, however,
because its couplet style represents nothing new in
Pope's handling of the couplet. The *Essay on Man* employs parallelism similar to that of *Windsor-Forest* and
balanced antithesis similar to that of the *Essay on Criticism* and *The Rape of the Lock*, but with the difference
that in the earlier poems Pope did not use series of open
lines with quite the same flexibility or with as many
changes of rhythm and shifts of design within his patterns of balance and parallelism. The *Epistle to Burling-*

ton represents and begins a different phase of Pope's couplet art, while the *Essay on Man*, brilliant and important as it is, does not.

Earl R. Wasserman has written of the "fine Roman aristocrat who stands behind the *Epistle to Burlington* and is responsible for the values governing it."[2] Reuben A. Brower has also noted the Roman character of the poem and has summarized the main modes of Pope's allusions:

> The Roman character of the voice is brought out through casual reference to the paraphernalia of ancient culture—'hecatombs, 'quincunxes,' and 'Tritons,' through pompous exclamations and commands associated with Roman satirical and prophetic styles, and finally by parody of various classical styles, heroic, pastoral-descriptive, and elegiac.[3]

The strength and value of Roman tradition is deepened too by Pope's concern with two great designers who were not Romans, but who adapted Roman models: Palladio, the Italian Renaissance master to whom Pope gives special attention, and Inigo Jones, who adapted Palladio to English uses and who was called "Vitruvius Britannicus" after the great ancient Roman architect. One of the most important patterns of allusion, however, is to Roman deities and sub-deities, which creates for the whole poem a mythic atmosphere and sense of presence to which all its particular scenes and descriptions are related.

Although Pope creates and uses a Roman stance and viewpoint, he does not let us forget that he is, nonetheless, a good eighteenth century Englishman, still Pope himself, often humorous and satirical, sometimes downright impish, but never scathing and bitter. The basis

from which Pope develops his poem is the contrast of
"magnificent" false taste with true taste, magnificent or
otherwise, which fuses the requirements of Nature with
those of human use. Since Pope's satiric task is to point
out instructive examples of bad taste, he acts as the
reader's (Burlington's) observer of the gardens and
buildings of the poem, and uses the guise of objective
description to make his satiric points. But the task of
persuading the reader is somewhat difficult because the
issue of the false use of riches is not one of deep immediate moral or personal involvement for writer or reader,
although the values at stake are of ultimate importance
for civilization. The reader must be firmly but gently
won, not shocked, outraged, or inspired, and to achieve
this persuasive end Pope employs some of his most successful comic verse and ingratiating satire.

The dominant couplet style of the *Epistle to Burlington*, one of Pope's shorter major poems, is a smoothly
flowing, rhythmical parallelism varied with couplets that
are just slightly formal and oratorical in accordance with
his Roman manner, but unpatterned as the ordinary
formal prose of Addison or Pope himself.

The opening paragraph, using the dominant style,
poses the basic question of why the prodigal recklessly
wastes his wealth to purchase "what he ne'er can taste":

> 'Tis strange, the Miser should his Cares employ,
> 2 To gain those Riches he can ne'er enjoy:
> Is it less strange, the Prodigal should wast
> 4 His wealth, to purchase what he ne'er can taste?
> Not for himself he sees, or hears, or eats;
> 6 Artists must chuse his Pictures, Music, Meats:
> He buys for Topham, Drawings and Designs,
> 8 For Pembroke Statues, dirty Gods, and Coins;
> Rare monkish Manuscripts for Hearne alone,

10 And Books for Meade, and Butterflies for Sloane.
  Think we all these are for himself? no more
12 Than his fine Wife, alas! or finer Whore.   (1–12)

Pope muses, asks and answers a question, and breaks out
at the end of the passage with a negative exclamation
that sets up a motif of prostitution which is related to
wealth and taste. " 'Tis strange," he reflects, and it is odd
that the antithesis of miser and prodigal comes merely to
a paradoxical similarity. The miser, as Pope shows in the
contemporaneous *Epistle to Bathurst*, suffers because he
is incapable of using the wealth he amasses, and the
prodigal is an inverted miser because he too cannot enjoy
or use what he wastes his wealth to buy. The rhyme of
the second couplet vibrates the problem of "waste" and
"taste," the two subjects of the poem. After the contrast
of miser and prodigal Pope shifts to a series of parallels
(6–10), concrete examples for the generalization of line
5, colored by "dirty," "monkish," and "Butterflies."
Then he turns from his rapid list to Burlington with a
question (11), rhetorical, yet sudden and direct; and in
contrast with his parallels, answers with the colloquial,
run-on line, capping the smooth weak "no more" with
the blunt, sudden "Whore." Even when he buys love,
the prodigal cannot enjoy it, just as he can neither buy,
nor enjoy, taste or true magnificence.

  Structurally there is nothing surprising here. But one
notices, just slightly, a loosening up, a mellowing of
earlier techniques. The antithesis of miser and prodigal
takes up two couplets, one a statement, the other a
question. In the first line Pope's typical inverted rhyme
thrust, "employ," comes out sharply; but the second
couplet employs natural order with a run-on line, and
the sharpness of the structural opposition is smoothed

out and muted. The last couplet with its question, its
run-on answer, the exclamation "alas," and with "finer
Whore" suddenly added as an afterthought, contrasts
the tight, parallel list, throwing its marching formality
awry with its blunt, colloquial contrast. This method of
easy shifts from brief passages of strict to looser parallelism, and from the thrusting rhyme inversion to a more
neutral structure in a colloquial tone dominates the
poem.

The thesis of the next paragraph is that Heaven visits
the wealthy fool with a taste, and Pope closes the passage
with the warning that, as a result of choosing the inept
Ripley as architect, Bubo is

> A standing sermon, at each year's expense,
> That never Coxcomb reach'd Magnificence!
>
> (21–22)

The nouns of this couplet gradually unlock the poem,
especially the climactic "Magnificence" which absorbs
the Aristotelian and Scholastic sense of liberality of ex-
penditure performed for good uses and in good taste.
Then to illustrate and to begin the development of these
resonant terms, Pope turns in the next line to the occasion at hand, to the effect of Burlington's publication of
*Fabriche Antiche designate da Andrea Palladio Vicen-
tino* (1730) upon coxcombs and wealthy fools:

> You show us, Rome was glorious, not profuse,
> 2 And pompous buildings once were things of Use.
> Yet shall (my Lord) your just, your noble rules
> 4 Fill half the land with Imitating Fools;
> Who random drawings from your sheets shall take,
> 6 And of one beauty many blunders make;
> Load some vain Church with old Theatric state,

8 Turn Archs of triumph to a Garden-gate;
  Reverse your Ornaments, and hang them all
10 On some patch'd dog-hole ek'd with ends of wall,
  Then clap four slices of Pilaster on't,
12 That lac'd with bits of rustic, makes a Front.
  Or call the winds thro' long Arcades to roar,
14 Proud to catch cold at a Venetian door;
  Conscious they act a true Palladian part,
16 And if they starve, they starve by rules of art.

(23–38)

Here are the parallel lines typical of Pope, and in the first two couplets, we do, indeed, get the effect of Wimsatt's statement that "no matter what their syntax, . . ." Pope's couplets "tend to hover on the verge of antithesis."[4] It is present in the rhymes but the syntax of the couplets is straight and neutral. The third couplet (5–6) tightens and points the syntax to emphasize the two key verbs, but without pivotal caesura. Then the easily swinging parallelism takes over, with one verb phrase after another, creating absurdities from one "beauty." In the first positions of lines 14 and 15, the parallels shift direction, dropping into the heavy adjectives and changing the rhythm of the meaning from action to condition; and in the final line, the parallels vary back to a double use of the verb "starve," with a conditional but literal emphasis upon the first and a psychological and satirical emphasis upon the second.

The design is actually rather strict; and Pope modulates from one kind of line to another only with "who" of line 5, with "Proud" of line 14, and with "if" of the final line to achieve the concluding satiric cadence. But in some ways the strict balance and parallelism has undergone a change since the *Essay on Criticism* and *The*

Rape of the Lock. Pope has radically decreased his use of
pivotal caesura as well as certain pairs of words which
create antithesis and balance, such as "none–each,"
"one–all," "neither–nor," "this–that," and so on, as well
as the use of "but" to pose a contrast. The syntax is more
direct and the strictness of design is less noticeable. The
line structures flow easily; and Pope creates a tone he is
not often allowed to have—a jovial disdain, a
good-natured contempt in key with the descriptive satire
characteristic of the poem rather than the tone of mol-
ten, punitive anger accented in other satires.

Up to this point Pope has posed the problem of why
the prodigal wastes his wealth "to purchase what he ne'er
can taste," and answered it only negatively and indirectly
with brief, generalized examples of three prodigals, and
passed, or rather come back, to a discussion of the occasion of the poem, sketching in quickly the results Burlington's "noble rules" will have. But there is method in
this indirect gambit, and now Pope is ready to go behind
the Palladian facades and "theatric state" of "imitating
fools" to examine the source of the distortion:

> Oft have you hinted to your brother Peer,
> A certain truth, which many buy too dear:
> Something there is more needful than Expence,
> And Something previous ev'n to Taste—'tis Sense:
> Good Sense, which only is the gift of Heav'n,
> And tho' no science, fairly worth the sev'n:
> A Light, which in yourself you must perceive;
> Jones and Le Nôtre have it not to give.   (39–46)

Given good sense, that inward light, the builder can then
cooperate with nature:

To build, to plant, whatever you intend,
To rear the Column, or the Arch to bend,
To swell the Terras, or to sink the Grot;
In all, let Nature never be forgot.
But treat the Goddess like a modest fair,
Nor over-dress, nor leave her wholly bare;
Let not each beauty ev'ry where be spy'd,
Where half the skill is decently to hide.
He gains all points, who pleasingly confounds,
Surprizes, varies, and conceals the Bounds.
    Consult the Genius of the Place in all;
That tells the Waters or to rise, or fall,
Or helps th' ambitious Hill the heav'n to scale,
Or scoops in circling theatres the Vale,
Calls in the Country, catches opening glades,
Joins willing woods, and varies shades from shades,
Now breaks or now directs, th' intending Lines;
Paints as you plant, and, as you work, designs.   (47–64)

An examination of some of the great eighteenth century houses and gardens still standing makes clear Pope's
meaning; and if some of the principles of garden and
landscape design which Pope favored are too symmetrical for contemporary tastes, they are at least much more
natural than the formal Dutch garden style of the late
seventeenth century which both Pope and Addison
thought too artificial. Pope's created garden and landscape has an organic quality; it operates more dynami-
cally upon the senses of sight and kinesthesia than the
geometric and ornate designs popular in the early years
of the eighteenth century.

The two passages above, which are continuous in the
poem, are a good example of Pope's basic contrast of
designs. The passage on sense withholds its two main
terms, "Sense" and "Light," until they have been strateg-

ically emphasized by appositives and subordinate clauses. In the second passage, the parallels of the first paragraph are varied with other structures. In the last paragraph, Pope uses only a series of verb phrases of carefully varied and textured sounds which describe the activities of the "Genius of the Place," that is, of Nature. In the last line Pope adds suddenly to these activities those of the artist and designer; and the parallels of the chiasmus express the cooperation of Nature and designer in a permanent and dynamic sense: "Paints as you plant, and, as you work, designs."

Then Pope shows the builder the result of his work if he has followed sense and has consulted the "Genius of the Place." "Sense," which we of the twentieth century so often think of as prosaic and practical, or Lockean and analytical, is raised by Pope to the level of "soul." The quality or character of a landscape or building is intangible to those without aesthetic perception, and Pope implies throughout that this perception must be founded on sense, that "Light which in yourself you must perceive." Thus only the dynamic fusion of sense, the soul of art, with Nature can create a work of lasting significance:

> Still follow Sense, of ev'ry Art the Soul,
> Parts answ'ring parts shall slide into a whole,
> Spontaneous beauties all around advance,
> Start ev'n from Difficulty, strike from Chance;
> Nature shall join you, Time shall make it grow
> A Work to wonder at—perhaps a STOW.   (65–70)

Pope clearly does not suggest that the builder use his art to remake nature according to a mathematical or mechanical scheme, but rather that he fuse the unpatterned but dynamic wildness of nature, the things-as-they-are of nature, with the demands of human use and expression. Gardens, like "pompous" buildings, are things of human use, and Pope's theory of landscaping and gardening can accommodate a kitchen garden as well as exotic shrubs and flowers.[5] But to measure Pope's conception against the actual design of eighteenth century gardens and landscapes, beautiful as many of them were, ultimately distorts his poem. Pope's garden and "place" is an ideal, and for this reason, always to be striven for. We could never, perhaps, agree about whether a particular eighteenth century "place" or garden—even Pope's own at Twickenham, if it were standing—answers his poetic theory of a garden fully or accurately; for his poem is more than even an interesting and humanistic document about eighteenth century taste. It describes an ideal twentieth century garden as well. Perhaps a contemporary builder or gardener could warmly agree with Pope's theory, but on the actualities of laying out a real garden, no doubt, he would differ sharply with Pope's plan for his landscape at Twickenham if it were known in detail, or with his "blueprint" for his famous grotto.[6] So the *Epistle to Burlington* is not a How-to-do-It piece about building and gardening written by a skilled amateur in 1731. It is firmly based in the real gardens of Pope's day, but it is a poem, and the garden or place is an ideal, an archetype. Just as in *Windsor-Forest* the forest as archetypal garden was an instance of *concordia discors*, so here, Pope's ordered landscape is an instance of *concordia discors* operating in an artistic way; for man's art cooperates with physical nature's power and sprawling discreteness by creating in the garden and landscape a smaller and refined example of nature in the large. The gardener and builder imitates but controls the harmonious strife of nature, confining it to a small space and time; but the harmonious tensions of the garden which man cultivates and controls are analogous to the cosmic tensions of nature under the law of *concordia discors.*

And now Pope moves to a couple of examples which are difficult at first glance to fit closely into the theme of the poem. First, Villario, who has worked long and spent much:

> Behold Villario's ten-years toil compleat;
> 2 His Quincunx darkens, his Espaliers meet,
>   The Wood supports the Plain, the parts unite,
> 4 And strength of Shade contends with strength of Light;
>   A waving Glow his bloomy beds display,
> 6 Blushing in bright diversities of day,
>   With silver-quiv'ring rills meander'd o'er—
> 8 Enjoy them, you! Villario can no more;
>   Tir'd of the scene Parterres and Fountains yield,
> 10 He finds at last he better likes a Field.   (79–88)

There is a hint of parody in lines 5–7; the over-fine diction tells us that Villario has overdone it just a bit—at least he is satiated with the scene he has worked on so long, so he turns with relief to a field. Why? Because he is a restless searcher after taste and good sense; he lacks sense, he planned wrong, incompletely, since Pope's lines imply that his place should have had the proper amount of field in it to begin with. Next, Sabinus is just at the point of happily watching his young woods burst into bloom with their branches longing to meet. His son, however, who inherits the beautiful scene, has other ideas:

> His Son's fine Taste an op'ner Vista loves,
> Foe to the Dryads of his Father's groves,
> One boundless Green, or flourish'd Carpet views,
> With all the mournful family of Yews;
> The thriving plants ignoble broomsticks made,
> Now sweep those Alleys they were born to shade.
>
> (93–98)

Much the same thing that was wrong with Villario is wrong with Sabinus' son. The son is cursed with uncertainty of taste, which is no taste at all, and he cannot rest content with the Dryads of his father's groves who represent the "Genius of the Place." In short, restlessness and uncertainty characterize Villario and Sabinus' son because they lacked sense, and as a result, could not achieve taste.

A rather famous piece of Pope's description, the picture of Timon's villa, contains some of his finest examples of imitative verse. In Pope's own note, this piece was "intended to comprize the principles of a false taste of magnificence." After a brief introduction of this "Brobdignag" (sic) of bad taste, Pope, our perceptive and eloquent guide, cries out:

> Lo, what huge heaps of littleness around!
> The whole, a labour'd Quarry above ground.
> Two Cupids squirt before: a Lake behind
> Improves the keenness of the Northern wind.
>
> (109–12)

With his surprised "Lo," Pope suggests that here is an enormous violation of the norm he has been talking about all along. He pauses, stares, and hangs the great,

awkward building in front of us, omitting the verbs in
the first couplet to emphasize the heavy ugliness of Timon's mansion; and in the next two lines makes an
active contrast to the "Quarry" in the sudden, direct
sentence, "Two Cupids squirt, . . ." with the unpleasant
urinary suggestion of "squirt." He continues, letting the
simple directness of his statement take full advantage of
the ironic play upon "improve," for which prodigals like
Timon court the gratitude and admiration of their visitors. Now Pope's keen eye roves over Timon's gardens:

> His Gardens next your admiration call,
> 2 On ev'ry side you look, behold the Wall!
> No pleasing Intricacies intervene,
> 4 No artful wildness to perplex the scene;
> Grove nods at grove, each Alley has a brother,
> 6 And half the platform just reflects the other.
> The suff'ring eye inverted Nature sees,
> 8 Trees cut to Statues, Statues thick as trees,
> With here a Fountain, never to be play'd,
> 10 And there a Summer-house, that knows no shade;
> Here Amphitrite sails thro' myrtle bow'rs;
> 12 There Gladiators fight, or die, in flow'rs;
> Un-water'd see the drooping sea-horse mourn,
> 14 And swallows roost in Nilus' dusty Urn.   (113-26)

It is perhaps superfluous to comment on this fine passage
except to notice the design of the passage as it moves
from statement (1–4), through expressive and representative mockery (5–8), to the sonorous melancholy of the
close. The stone gladiators dying in flowers add a touch
of ludicrous pathos, and "Nilus' dusty Urn," with its
marmoreal and classical suggestions, comes with a dying
fall upon the other classical suggestions in the passage.
Timon's magnificence is a showy perversion of use and

taste; the delicate sea horse sickens and the fountains are clogged with bird roosts.

And now our guide sees the great man strutting, waiting for his guests to arrive:

> My Lord advances with majestic mein,
> 2 Smit with the mighty pleasure, to be seen:
> But soft—by regular approach—not yet—
> 4 First thro' the length of yon hot Terrace sweat,
> And when up ten steep slopes you've dragg'd your
>   thighs,
> 6 Just at his Study-door he'll bless your eyes.   (127–32)

This little incident is rendered with wry and disdainful humor. The emphatic "smit" of the inverted first foot of line 2 makes a sudden emphasis; and the limping conclusion, "to be seen," exhibits Timon forcefully, since the heavy phrase, "be seen," contrasts the pyhrric foot preceding it. The colloquial third line with its two heavy pauses dramatizes the action. All three final lines are inverted; but there is no hint of artificiality because the diction is plain and colloquial, and except for "Terrace" and "Study," all the words are monosyllables. In the penultimate line, the "ten low words" suggest "creeping."⁷ The line looks longer, the reader tends to slow down, for the harsh "dragg'd" suggests the sense of the effort described. Quickly in the last line, the inverted "just at his Study-door," prepares for the appearance of Timon who suddenly—looking pompous—overwhelms the exasperated visitor. Pope's language seems direct, natural, colloquial, but in the last three lines he inverts three prepositional phrases. "Sweat" is forceful and we notice it as an inversion, but we are hardly aware of the inverted prepositional phrases. Only inversions of

subject–verb and of verb–object strike one as unnatural
order, but when they occur in lines of simple, monosyllabic words, the inverted order is muted. Pope makes inverted order sound direct and natural by submerging and
de-emphasizing it with contrasting effects, a measure
here of the growth of his skill in making his couplet seem
unpretentious, colloquial, and lithely expressive of a situation or scene.

Next the visitors gape in my Lord's study as he shows
them the fancy bindings of Du Sueil and the printing of
Aldus Manutio.[8] Our more penetrating and observant
guide sees, however, that many of the books are merely
false wooden backs, and that two great authors of the
recent past, Milton and Locke, are nowhere to be found
(133–40). Then the "tour" ends with chapel:

> And now the Chapel's silver bell you hear,
> That summons you to all the Pride of Pray'r:
> Light quirks of Musick, broken and uneven,
> Make the soul dance upon a Jig to Heaven.
> On painted Cielings you devoutly stare,
> Where sprawl the Saints of Verrio or Laguerre,
> On gilded clouds in fair expansion lie,
> And bring all Paradise before your eye.
> To rest, the Cushion and soft Dean invite,
> Who never mentions Hell to ears polite.   (141–50)

The work of the two painters Pope mentions is rather
florid, second-rate Baroque, precisely the quality the lines
suggest. The easy straightforward movement lulls the
reader comfortably, but the diction jars, working against
the design. There is a wildly humorous quality about the
soul dancing a jig to heaven. Pope stares, solemnly pre-
tending to be devout in spite of the sensuous, sprawling

saints floating upon their gilded clouds, as a sumptuous and tawdry paradise opens before them. The opening paradise is followed nicely by "To rest"; and the verb, "invite," finally comes to state what the lines suggest, and to characterize the oleaginous dean, who, in the climactic, ironic subordinate clause, is too "polite" to break the complacency of his "audience."

No sooner is the chapel service over than,

> But hark! the chiming Clocks to dinner call;
> A hundred footsteps scrape the marble Hall:
> The rich Buffet well-colour'd Serpents grace,
> And gaping Tritons spew to wash your face.
>
> (151–54)

Except for the opening interjection, four lines make four simple, declarative statements. There is no balance and no caesura. Pope concentrates carefully on the sound quality in these simple structures to suggest with "Hark" and "call–Hall" the reverberating hollowness of the great marble room, and with the tightening of the broad back vowels to front, closed vowels in the second couplet, the nasty effect of painted snakes and spewing statues. The keenness of the guest's appetite, unless perverted like the decor of the dining room, is hardly "improved."

Immediately Pope breaks from his description and generalizes harshly, calling the dining room a temple and a hecatomb (155–58). The frightened waiters serve the courses on rigorous schedule without regard to the guests' desire for comfort and geniality:

> So quick retires each flying course, you'd swear
> Sancho's dread Doctor and his Wand were there.
>
> (159–60)

Then the mockery of the poem is over, and Pope drops
to bald, disdainful statement:

> In plenty starving, tantaliz'd in state,
> And complaisantly help'd to all I hate,
> Treated, caress'd, and tir'd, I take my leave
> Sick of his civil Pride from Morn to Eve;
> I curse such lavish cost, and little skill,
> And swear no Day was ever past so ill.   (163–68)

The chiastic opening line is the kind of natural chiasmus
a man might speak under the stress of the emotion Pope
feels. He continues boldly, simply showing the sudden
collapse of his satiric stance: one gets tired of being
sarcastic at Timon's expense, one is finally overwhelmed
and disgusted, and one wants to get out. But after the
frustration of his visit, he suddenly qualifies his satire,
and sees through and beyond the waste and magnificence
of Timon's villa a restorative vision of Nature:

>   Yet hence the Poor are cloath'd, the Hungry fed;
> 2 Health to himself, and to his Infants bread
>   The Lab'rer bears: What his hard heart denies,
> 4 His charitable Vanity supplies.
>   Another age shall see the golden Ear
> 6 Imbrown the Slope, and nod on the Parterre,
>   Deep Harvests bury all his pride has plann'd
> 8 And laughing Ceres re-assume the land.
>
>   (169–76)

The slowed tempo and the quiet tone of the first paragraph contrast the incisiveness of the satire against
Timon and his villa and the hard scorn of Pope's depar-
ture. Its two balanced parallels, the second of which (2)
is a chiasmus, and its concluding balanced antithesis give
it an underlying symmetry of structure which is vital to

its theme; but the enjambment of line 2, and the division of the last sentence with the inversion of the long, periphrastic object, "What his hard heart denies," create an effect of imbalanced ruggedness from the underlying symmetry. Then the design of the second paragraph takes over to complete the theme in a different movement. The first line (5) gives us the key verb, "see," and the design is simply three parallels flowing from this verb. The run-on "Imbrown," a curiously restrained verb, accurately suggests the slow ripening of a grain field. The last line is the climactic one of the satirical and descriptive parts of the poem. "Laughing Ceres" (literally a waving field of grain gleaming in the sun) "imbrowns" the slope and "re-assumes" the land. She is the queen restored who remounts her rightful throne of Nature which has been violated and trampled by Timon. "Laughing Ceres," one of Pope's finest personifications, is effective because the concrete generality of his language suggests two complementary meanings working at the same time: the realm of literal nature and the realm of myth, and Pope has unassumingly but carefully supported this relationship. All along, the Nature which builders and planners such as Timon have been "improving" has been something that is alive and vital with purposes of its own, which, however, yields to proper human cultivation and partnership. Nature is called a "Goddess" (51); each place and scene has its "Genius" (57); and groves are inhabited by "Dryads" (94). The poetic assumption of mythological presences suggests a spiritual quality; and when "laughing Ceres" remounts her throne, the land is not only returned to an unpretentious, practical human use, but to a normality in tune with cosmic process and purpose.

Since Timon is typical of the prodigal, Pope asks:

> Who then shall grace, or who improve the Soil?
> Who plants like BATHURST, or who builds like BOYLE.
> 'Tis Use alone that sanctifies Expence,
> And Splendor borrows all her rays from Sense. (177–80)

Clearly the metaphoric and transcendent implications of building and planting are driven home by Pope's probable play upon the religious associations of "grace," by the "sanctification" of expense, and by splendor's borrowed rays. After a paragraph emphasizing the generosity and usefulness of the ideal builder and planter (182–90), Pope ends the poem in lines less interesting than the rest of the poem but which are fitting. Burlington is called upon in sweeping, imperative parallels:

> You too proceed! make falling Arts your care,
> Erect new wonders, and the old repair,
> Jones and Palladio to themselves restore,
> And be whate'er Vitruvius was before:
> Till Kings call forth th' idea's of your mind,
> Proud to accomplish what such hands design'd,
> Bid Harbors open, public Ways extend,
> Bid Temples, worthier of the God, ascend;
> Bid the broad Arch the dang'rous Flood contain,
> The Mole projected break the roaring Main;
> Back to his bounds their subject Sea command,
> And roll obedient Rivers thro' the Land;
> These Honours, peace to happy Britain brings,
> These are Imperial Works, and worthy Kings.
>
> (191–204)

The imperative mood of the whole ending tells us that this great vision of man working in ideal harmony with Nature is by no means realized, it is merely a hope.

Making this vision a reality is worthy of kings; and Pope sees Burlington waiting for the ideal king, who like "laughing Ceres" will "re-assume" and clarify a realm of building and gardening to which the misuse of riches by bad taste has brought disorder and deformity.

The *Epistle to Burlington* lacks the scathing satire of Pope's great manner in the *Imitations of Horace*, the depth and sublety of the *Epistle to Bathurst*, the range and power of the *Dunciad*; but beneath its casual manner Pope's intense appreciation of Nature's relations to man's art in the production of fruitful and pleasing order is created in a poetic and persuasive way. We have seen how ingratiatingly the norm of building and planting has been given, a dynamic norm with possibility of variation, one which appeals to a basic but ideal desire to cooperate with Nature in order to significantly identify with it. The violations and distortions of this norm by the coxcomb, the pretender to taste, and the prodigal are rendered graphically and objectively. After giving the reader an ideal with which it would be difficult to quarrel, Pope conducts him through Timon's villa, and his poetic vision, as well as his sharp senses, misses nothing. His frequent interjections, his guise of objective description, and his snatches of comic verse show the reader the effect of bad architecture and gardens upon an ideal observer. And toward the end when Pope turns, weary and disgusted, from Timon's place to a vision of fields of grain waving above the crumbled mansion, he has brought the reader with him to a final identification with Nature as a dynamic ideal that must be observed with reverence and used with sense.

The *Epistle to Burlington* flows with such casual grace that the reader is hardly aware of its variations of couplet structure and stylistic design. Pope's sentences fall into parallels half the time; and the other half of the time, the couplet structures are as varied as ordinary prose. Pope touches his dominant, fluid parallelism and his neutral designs with a little, but just enough, balanced antithesis and chiasmus to suggest, and sometimes to comically represent, the inversion and distortion of the poem's ideal of harmony. As in *Windsor-Forest*, parallelism controls and dominates antithesis. Like *Windsor-Forest*, too, the *Epistle to Burlington* is, to a great extent, a descriptive poem, but the adjectives are never obtrusive as they sometimes are in *Windsor-Forest* and the other early poems. When antithesis and balance is used in line against line, or in half-line against half-line, the grammatical or syntactic form of the first part of the parallel is repeated in some way, or its repetition is suggested by some form of compression or elision; and when description is used with a great deal of balance, as in the poems before *The Rape of the Lock*, the adjectives quickly become stiff and monotonous even when they are functional and not merely decorative. What has happened in the *Epistle to Burlington* as well as in the *Dunciad*, is that Pope has concentrated more upon the sentence as the unit of composition and less upon the line and half-line. The sentence of the present poem, one can notice quickly, is a simpler, more straightforward one than that of the *Dunciad's* norm. The forms of subordination are less extended and complex. When the narrator uses a great deal of subordination, as in *Eloisa to Abelard* and the *Dunciad*, he creates a more complex image of himself; but Pope's point of view in the *Epistle to Burlington* is radically different. Given the subject matter of the poem—gardens, landscapes, and houses—

Pope's objectifying his theme by observing and reacting to his subject matter is more effective than the working out of an extended dialectic or the use of a complex satiric and personal involvement. The style of the present poem picks up the subject and examines it, sticks to it and identifies with it, whether Pope grows warm for three or four lines of flowing parallels, registers his satiric astonishment by describing Timon's villa, or quietly catches a vision of the goddess Ceres.

NOTES

1. The background of the publication of the *Epistle to Burlington* is found in *Twick. Ed.* III–ii, 2nd ed. (1961) *Epistles to Several Persons*, ed. F. W. Bateson, Introduction, pp. ix–xxiii, and in *Twick. Ed.* III–i (1950) *An Essay on Man*, ed. Maynard Mack, Introduction, pp. xi–xiv.

2. *Pope's Epistle to Bathurst: A Critical Reading with an Edition of the Manuscripts* (Baltimore, The Johns Hopkins Press, 1960), p. 11.

3. *Alexander Pope: The Poetry of Allusion*, p. 244.

4. *The Verbal Icon*, p. 158.

5. Maynard Mack, " 'The Shadowy Cave': Some Speculation on a Twickenham Grotto," *Restoration and Eighteenth Century Literature: Essays in Honor of Alan Dugald McKillop* (Chicago: University of Chicago Press, 1963), pp. 69–70.

6. For Pope's plans for his grotto, see Benjamin Boyce, "Mr. Pope, in Bath, Improves the Design of His Grotto," *Restoration and Eighteenth Century Literature: Essays in Honor of Alan Dugald McKillop* (Chicago: University of Chicago Press, 1963), pp. 143–53.

7. I am using Pope's own words about the improper use of monosyllables, in the *Essay on Criticism*, 1. 347.

8. See *Twick. Ed.*, III–ii, note 136, p. 150.

9

The Epilogue to the Satires 1738

BETWEEN THE *Epistle to Burlington* in 1731 and the *Epilogue to the Satires* in 1738, Pope published the three remaining *Moral Essays* or "Epistles to Several Persons," as he called them, the *Essay on Man*, and the *Imitations of Horace*, among which *The Epistle to Dr. Arbuthnot* and the *Epilogue to the Satires* are Horatian in certain ways, but have no parallels in Horace. In these Horatian poems, the couplet style begun in the *Epistle to Burlington* is carried forward and developed in accordance with the themes and viewpoints of the poems. In many ways the *Epistle to Dr. Arbuthnot* is the most brilliant, and certainly the most popular, of all these poems; and in it, Pope employs with unfailing artistry a dazzling variety of stylistic modes. His couplet norm in this poem is an utterly direct, simple couplet of varied structure that achieves its wit and satiric effect without his characteristic balance and antithesis, a norm almost the same as that of the *Epilogue*; but against this norm Pope plays several varieties of antithesis and balance, such as the famous "Portrait of Atticus" (193–214). One of the distinctive characteristics of the *Epistle to Dr. Arbuthnot*, the "Prologue to the Satires," is its conversational

tone and frequent easy colloquialism. Ever since the
Essay on Criticism Pope had shown that he could make
the couplet reflect conversational rhythms, but it is in
the Horatian poems that this quality receives its fullest
and maturest development. In the *Epistle to Dr. Arbuthnot* Pope makes the couplet reflect many different tones
and modes of speech, creating a wide range of comic and
satiric effects which defines and expresses his role as a
special kind of satirist: witty, cultivated, insouciant, yet
also simple and genial, the *Vir Bonum* caught in the
world of duncery and striking back with all his great
resources of wit and imagination. Pope employs parallelism similar to that of the *Epistle to Burlington,* and
a couplet norm similar to the dominant style of the *Epilogue;* but the distinctive passages and the paragraphs of
the *Epilogue* are different from those of either poem. For
these reasons, I consider the *Epilogue* next because it illustrates better than the *Epistle to Dr. Arbuthnot* the
final development of Pope's couplet art.

In the *Epistle to Dr. Arbuthnot* Pope was trium-
phantly confident of his ability to punish, and by punish-
ing, to dispose of his victims; he was even entertained by
the literary spectacle that he satirized. But in the *Epilogue* things are different. Pope senses imminent cata-
strophe. Expecting to be silenced by the law of the land,
he feels almost alone in his attack upon the enveloping
forces of vice. And unlike his role as Satirist in the
Dunciad, he is not a prophet overwhelmed by a cataclys-
mic vision of the triumph of Dulness, but an angry
satirist, defender and champion of what little is left of
honesty and virtue. Clothed in his integrity and power of
utterance, he stands forth against a corrupt world and
dares it to silence him.

Pope develops the two dialogues which form the poem by dramatizing in each his contest with a "Friend," an adversary who provokes the Satirist and reproaches him all the way. In a note to the first poem Pope explains that he means the Friend to be an "impertinent censurer," and the Friend is that and something more. Although cynical, complacent, and a creature, body and soul, of the court and fashionable opinion, he is, nonetheless, a strong adversary since Pope has done the artistic justice of making him glib and tenacious, even able to indulge in satire of his own (I. 87–104).[1] The first Dialogue begins informally with a friendly, patronizing speech by the Friend advising Pope to write with more rapture and with less morality, to go slow, to be more general in his satire, to compromise like a reasonable man, to flatter those in power, and to aim his pen at eccentrics or at those out of power or fashion so that everybody can be in comfortably on the Satirist's jokes at their expense. But Pope believes in speaking the truth boldly. Knowing his Friend for what he is, ironic and amused at his moral obtuseness, he destroys with offhand finesse, sometimes by the indirect method of interrogation, every demurrer that the Friend advances. But this is only the initial confrontation of attitudes from which the poem develops. Amoral and detached about any real issues of right or wrong, the Friend continues to urge as right the attractive, expedient sway of fashionable opinion until Pope is finally goaded out of his ironic stance and turns with fierce and eloquent sarcasm not upon the Friend personally but upon the meretriciousness and smugness of the whole society which the Friend speaks for.

The developing counterpoint of the *Epilogue* is very

different from the rhetorical progression of the *Epistle to Dr. Arbuthnot.* The *Epilogue* grows out of the opposing assumptions of Pope and his censurer about the proper relation of satire to its object and to its audience, which ultimately becomes for Pope a question of right and wrong. The antagonists feel each other out, feinting at each other's position until they finally face each other in the open. Pope handles the Friend differently than he handled Dr. Arbuthnot, who, in spite of his function as encourager and sounding board, is relatively passive because the form of the two poems is different: the *Epistle* is almost a dramatic monologue, but the two poems of the *Epilogue* are really dialogues,[2] for Pope's theme and satiric focus is developed in response to the variously couched argument of the Friend for a type of satire that is general, entertaining and harmless. Toward Arbuthnot, his real friend, and a noted public figure, Pope is respectful and gracious; with the Friend, he is more outspoken. The two men do not respect each other, we feel the aggravating nearness and tenacity of the Friend, and Pope treats him appropriately with bantering contempt.

A passage close to the beginning of *Dialogue I* will illustrate the *Epilogue's* informality and the proselike fluidity of its couplets. The Friend has already opened by charging Pope with "decay of parts," with excessive concern for morality, and with stealing from Horace. He continues in the lines below, growing slightly exasperated, as he thinks of Horace's delicacy and Pope's bluntness:

> But *Horace*, Sir, was delicate, was nice;
> *Bubo* observes, he lash'd no sort of *Vice:*

Horace would say, *Sir* Billy *serv'd the Crown,*
Blunt *could do Bus'ness,* H—ggins *knew the Town,*
In *Sappho* touch the *Failing of the Sex,*
In rev'rend Bishops note some *small Neglects,*
And own, the *Spaniard* did a *waggish thing,*
Who cropt our Ears, and sent them to the King.
His sly, polite, insinuating stile
Could please at Court, and make AUGUSTUS smile:
An artful Manager, that crept between
His Friend and Shame, and was a kind of *Screen.*
But 'faith your very Friends will soon be sore;
Patriots there are, who wish you'd jest no more—
And where's the Glory? 'twill be only thought
The Great man never offer'd you a Groat.
Go see Sir ROBERT—
                      P.   See Sir ROBERT!—hum—
And never laugh—for all my life to come?
                                               (11–28)

The linear syntax, the quiet rhyming, and the run-on's
fuse to conceal the satiric pitfalls lurking under the simple surface. The ordinary techniques of sentence structure and continuity are simple and varied, and the
rhymes fall upon different parts of speech. They lack the
bold and witty contrasts which depend upon parallelism,
but they carry an oblique wit. Those of the first couplet
make an oddly ironic contrast. The second rhyme,
"*Crown–Town,*" is neutral and parallel; the third,
"*Sex–Neglects,*" is a correlative which mingles "*Sappho*"
and "Bishops" in a naughty aura; "*waggish thing*" jars in
front of "King," as the casual brutality of the Jenkins'
Ear affair is brought up; the Horatian "stile" the Friend
wants and which Pope will not give, ironically creates
Augustus' "Smile." The causal relation of "between"
and "*Screen*" is particularly odd, since what the Friend
really thinks Pope should be in his role as satirist–poet is

a "screen" that "creeps." "Sore" and "no more" creates a negative cause–effect relation. A "Groat" is a cheap iron coin, but how ironic it is that a "Groat" is really what the "thought" is worth that the Friend ascribes to the public mind. And in the last couplet, the rhymes rather wittily break down, as Pope muses and "hums" a moment about the consequences of getting entangled in the web of the greatest politician on earth, Sir Robert Walpole. What Pope shows with this type of rhyming, as he increasingly demonstrates after *The Rape of the Lock*, is that he does not need either pointed balance and parallelism, either chiasmus or zeugma, to make rhymes that are freighted with wit. If a poem is one in which a particular kind of balance or parallelism is dominant and thematic, then the rhymes will obey and reinforce the pattern and character of the lines. In the *Epilogue* this is not the case, for balance and parallelism is a very minor feature of the poem. The informal, offhand manner of the lines, rather oily and confidential at this point, characterize the Friend who is unintentionally witty because he is cynical, morally obtuse, and, in spite of his chattering and superficial acquaintance with Horace, ignorant of this great writer's real importance. In Pope's replies, he sometimes mimics the Friend in the same kind of style, but he also contrasts this style in the rhythmic peaks of the satire.

The Friend continues his argument, and later gives Pope the cynical advice to "spread wide the ridicule, and charitably comfort Knave and Fool." And Pope replies in a different mode from the passage above:

> P.   Dear Sir, forgive the Prejudice of Youth:
> 2 Adieu Distinction, Satire, Warmth, and Truth!
> Come harmless *Characters* that no one hit,

4 Come *Henley*'s Oratory, *Osborn*'s Wit!
　The Honey dropping from *Favonio*'s tongue,
6 The Flow'rs of *Bubo*, and the Flow of Y—*ng!*
　The gracious Dew of Pulpit Eloquence;
8 And all the well-whipt Cream of Courtly Sense,
　That first was H—*vy*'s, F—'s next, and then
10 The S—te's, and then H—*vy*'s once agen.
　O come, that easy *Ciceronian* stile,
12 So *Latin*, yet so *English* all the while,
　As, tho' the Pride of *Middleton* and *Bland*,
14 All Boys may read, and Girls may understand!
　Then might I sing without the least Offence,
16 And all I sung should be the *Nation's Sense*:
　Or teach the melancholy Muse to mourn,
18 Hang the sad Verse on CAROLINA'S URN,
　And hail her passage to the Realms of Rest,
20 All Parts perform'd, and *all* her Children blest!
　So—Satire is no more—I feel it die—
22 No *Gazeteer* more innocent than I!
　And let, a God's-name, ev'ry Fool and Knave
24 Be grac'd thro' Life, and flatter'd in his Grave.
                                           (I. 63–86)

Pope mocks forms of popular eloquence and style; and
down through the lines on Queen Caroline's children
(20) suggests with his hackneyed poeticisms the language of his victims, embodied in parallel and compounding lines that create an effect of sonorous sarcasm.
Then without transition, a change of diction and change
of rhythm with "So—Satire is no more—," and the passage comes to its end with a shocking directness and
concision of design contrasting the parodic poetry in the
soaring design of the previous lines. This type of movement is a favorite of Pope's after *Windsor-Forest*, and is
especially appropriate to satire where the more preten-
tious and surface aspect of a situation is given, and then

in the concluding lines is stripped away or destroyed to reveal the real rather than the apparent truth. The difference between this passage and most of the *Epistle to Burlington* and the *Epistle to Dr. Arbuthnot* is that these twenty-four lines contain no balanced antithesis, no recoiling or chiastic syntax, and its small amount of parallelism is neutral.

Dialogue I plays back and forth between the insistent demand of his adversary that Pope write harmless satire entertaining to the court, and Pope's varied modes of ironic refusal. In his final speech (I. 87–104), the Friend insists with characteristic cynicism that satire must "know its time and place," and that it attack the Great only when they fall. At this point (105–22) Pope turns on the Friend because he will not see that if satire is to have strength and worth, it must attack those who deserve attack, no matter who or where they are. But with an effective ironic reversal, Pope attacks not the Friend, not the aristocracy, but those who, lacking the appearance of titles and wealth, presume to sin like their betters. Warming to his irony, Pope grows more intense, moves to his coda and creates an emblematic picture of a nation enthralled and enslaved by the worship of vice. These are the concluding lines and the answer to the Friend:

> *Vice* is undone, if she forgets her Birth,
> And stoops from Angels to the Dregs of Earth:
> But 'tis the *Fall* degrades her to a Whore;
> Let *Greatness* own her, and she's mean no more:
> Her Birth, her Beauty, Crowds and Courts confess,
> Chaste Matrons praise her, and grave Bishops bless:
> In golden Chains the willing World she draws,
> And hers the Gospel is, and hers the Laws:

Mounts the tribunal, lifts her scarlet head,
And sees pale Virtue carted in her stead!
Lo! at the Wheels of her Triumphal Car,
Old *England's* Genius, rough with many a Scar,
Dragg'd in the Dust! his Arms hang idly round,
His Flag inverted trails along the ground!
Our Youth, all liv'ry'd o'er with foreign Gold,
Before her dance; behind her crawl the Old!
See thronging Millions to the Pagod run,
And offer Country, Parent, Wife, or Son!
Hear her black Trumpet thro' the Land proclaim,
That 'Not to be corrupted is the Shame.'
In Soldier, Churchman, Patriot, Man in Pow'r,
'Tis Av'rice all, Ambition is no more!
See, all our Nobles begging to be Slaves!
See, all our Fools aspiring to be Knaves!
The Wit of Cheats, the Courage of a Whore,
Are what ten thousand envy and adore.
All, all look up, with reverential Awe,
On Crimes that scape, or triumph o'er the Law:
While Truth, Worth, Wisdom, daily they decry—
'Nothing is Sacred now but Villany.'

　　Yet may this Verse (if such a Verse remain)
　　Show there was one who held it in disdain.　(I. 141–72)

This fortissimo intensity approaches that of the close of
the fourth book of the *Dunciad*. Nothing matters but
the intense, unadorned rendering of the vision. Most of
the rhymes are neutral, the couplets closed and
end-stopped, and the sentences therefore short. Eleven
lines have no caesura at all, five have more than one
pause, and three have the main pause on the first sylla-
ble. As a result, there is no lilt depending on the movement to and from the medial caesura as there is in the
early poems in lines such as these:

> 'Tis hard to say if greater Want of Skill,
> Appear in *writing* or in *Judging* ill;
> But of the two, less dang'rous is th' Offence
> To tire our *Patience*, than mis-lead our *Sense*.
> (Essay on Criticism, 1–4)

> Thy Forests, *Windsor!* and thy green Retreats,
> At once the Monarch's and the Muse's Seats,
> Invite my Lays. Be present, Sylvan Maids!
> Unlock your Springs, and open all your Shades.
> (Windsor-Forest, 1–4)

The rhythms of the conclusion of *Dialogue I* are rougher, more irregular than these parallels. The scarcity of pivotal caesura and the wide variation of pauses enables Pope to use a more irregular meter. Lines without syntactic and metrical caesura often seem more energetic and intense (although this depends on the context and pattern of accent); for lines with strong medial caesuras separating two clauses or phrases often make the voice fall twice according to a more or less regular pattern. The lines of the conclusion of *Dialogue I* above move straight to the rhymes without the complications of balanced recoil; and in the concluding half of the passage, the rhymes blast out like trumpets. This passage differs as much from a passage of balanced lines in the *Pastorals* as it does from blank verse, and in either case the difference is considerable. The concluding couplet, a quiet one by contrast, illustrates a tendency of Pope's rhyming in his last poems. "Remain," ordinarily a weak rhyme word, is thrown in with deadly emphasis which climaxes much of what the Dialogue is about: such satire as Pope is writing may not indeed "remain," since the society he has just satirized may not allow it to. And then, of course, the concluding word, "disdain," reinforces the uncompromising scorn of the whole piece.

Dialogue II, a variation and development of *Dialogue I*, is the most memorable and disinterested tribute in English literature to the power and worth of great satire. Pope takes up more concretely the issues raised in *Dialogue I* because the Friend (Adversary) in this dialogue is not as clever and agile as the first Friend, and the Satirist must be more pointed and graphic in his treatment of certain issues. Pope's contention in *Dialogue I*, that satire must be specific, is brought home in the second dialogue with a brilliance and incisiveness that frightens the Adversary. *Dialogue I* opened with the Adversary comparing Pope with Horace, much to Pope's discredit. The opening of *Dialogue II* considers the question raised in *Dialogue I* of "lashing no sort of Vice" as opposed to attacking specific offenders:

> *Fr.* 'Tis all a Libel—*Paxton* (Sir) will say. ⎱
> 2 *P.* Not yet my Friend! to-morrow 'faith it may; ⎰
>   And for that very cause I print to day.
> 4 How shou'd I fret, to mangle ev'ry line,
>   In rev'rence to the Sins of *Thirty-nine!*
> 6 Vice with such Giant-strides comes on amain,
>   Invention strives to be before in vain;
> 8 Feign what I will, and paint it e'er so strong,
>   Some rising Genius sins up to my Song.
> 10 *F.* Yet none but you by Name the Guilty lash;
>   Ev'n *Guthry* saves half *Newgate* by a Dash.
> 12 Spare then the Person, and expose the Vice.
>   *P.* How Sir! not damn the Sharper, but the Dice?
> 14 Come on then Satire! gen'ral, unconfin'd,
>   Spread thy broad wing, and sowze on all the Kind.
> 16 Ye Statesmen, Priests, of one Religion all!
>   Ye Tradesmen vile, in Army, Court, or Hall!

18 Ye Rev'rend Atheists!—*F.* Scandal! name them, Who?
    P.   Why that's the thing you bid me not to do.
20 Who starv'd a Sister, who forswore a Debt,
    I never nam'd—the Town's enquiring yet.
22 The pois'ning Dame—*Fr.* You mean—*P.* I don't—*Fr.*
    You do.
    P.   See! now I keep the Secret, and not you.
24 The bribing Statesman—*Fr.* Hold! too high you go.
    P.   The brib'd Elector—*Fr.* There you stoop too
    low.
26 *P.*   I fain wou'd please you, if I knew with what:
    Tell me, which Knave is lawful Game, which not?
                           (II. 1–27)

These lines almost defy one to see a patterned design.
They are so simple, straightforward, and varied that
there is, in fact, no patterned repetition of line structure
that Pope employs earlier. Yet the integrity of the couplet is as firm as ever, for each is closed and end-stopped,
and the rhymes are strong without being obtrusive. They
lack Pope's earlier, typical criss-crossing analytical wit,
and the parallelism is neutral. To line 13, when Pope
begins putting pressure on the Friend, the rhymes make
an ironic equation in "strong–Song"; an odd resemblance in "lash–Dash," where the dash by which Guthry
omits the names of criminals resembles the mark left by
the "whip" of Satire; and a logical resemblance in
"Vice–Dice," where dice is a kind of vice. From this
point to the end, the rhymes are neutral and are absorbed by the exigencies of the dialogue as the Friend
takes the Satirist's bait, revealing in his confusion that he
must agree with Pope, or else admit that his assumptions
about the function of satire are worthless. Pope uses even
less inversion in the *Epilogue* than in the other late
Horatian satires, in the passage above, only in lines 10,

20–21, and 24. The inversions give to the informal whole just the slightest suggestion of formality, of deliberate patterning, to put some emphasis on the rhymes and to prevent the couplets from growing too loose or too informal.

The knife is in, and now Pope twists it slightly:

> Suppose I censure—you know what I mean—
> To save a Bishop, may I name a Dean?
>   *Fr.*   A Dean, Sir? no: his Fortune is not made,
> You hurt a man that's rising in the Trade.
>
> (II. 32–35)

In the first couplet Pope uses the anacoluthon with fine effect, changing the direction in the second line to a dilemma in tight parallels. These simple lines have a spontaneous and conversational quality, yet the iambic as well as the couplet form is strictly held. But as most undergraduates can demonstrate, the slightest overemphasis of the iambic destroys the proper expression of mordant, sly irony on Pope's part and the fatuous cynicism of the reply.

Later Pope refers to a passage in *Dialogue I* in which he mocked the literary sycophancy of the court as the "well-whipt cream of courtly sense." In *Dialogue II* the application is metaphoric but is made more concrete and less literary for a Friend who might not understand such things as literary plagiarism and Ciceronian style:

>   *P.*   Faith it imports not much from whom it came ⎫
> Whoever borrow'd, could not be to blame,   ⎬
> Since the whole House did afterwards the same: ⎭
> Let Courtly Wits to Wits afford supply,
> As Hog to Hog in Huts of *Wesphaly*;

If one, thro' Nature's Bounty or his Lord's,
Has what the frugal, dirty soil affords,
From him the next receives it, thick or thin,
As pure a Mess almost as it came in;
The blessed Benefit, not there confin'd,
Drops to the third who nuzzles close behind;
From tail to mouth, they feed, and they carouse;
The last, full fairly gives it to the *House.*
   Fr.   This filthy Simile, this beastly Line,
Quite turns my Stomach—*P.*   So does Flatt'ry mine;
And all your Courtly Civet–Cats can vent,
Perfume to you, to me is Excrement.

(II. 168–184)

This is an undeniably rank and earthy passage couched in the language of a simile, but its implications go beyond the limits of most similes to achieve a striking metaphoric force. It is impersonal, and Pope asks the reader to see the literary fawning and imitative flattery of the court and the parliament for what it really is. There are almost no features of design that can be isolated, as is the case of so much of the *Epilogue.* The rhymes, again, contain no antithetic and alogical resemblances, but act as reinforcers of the sense, for they create, rather than any kind of surprise, an exactness of emphasis. On the surface, "came–blame–same," "thin–in," and "confin'd–behind," appear to be weak rhymes since they are mostly adverbs and adjectives, but when one looks at the sense of the passage, their satiric nicety and exactness supports the simple, straightforward lines which understate the gross scatology of the content. But Pope's powerful simile of the fashionable and courtly literary pig pen employs no unpolite or improper words; and the reader's imagination is all that is necessary. The oblique and witty parallels are gone, as are the massed and con-

trasted structural designs. Pope depends on the graphic
image stated simply.

It is clear throughout both Dialogues that Pope's role
as Satirist is different than in the *Epistle to Dr. Arbuthnot* and in the other Horatian poems. His situation as
Satirist is more dramatic in its involvement with his two
adversaries; and while maintaining his sense of magnificent irony, he is more desperate and intense. His back is
to the wall and at this point he will not waste the
playfulness of his wit on a totally corrupt society. All
that wit is used for in the *Epilogue* is to parry each
Friend, though with a different ironic mode in each
dialogue, until it becomes necessary to bury his amoral-
ity, his viciousness or his obtuseness with an intense and
eloquent barrage of scornful irony.

Toward the end of *Dialogue II* when Pope tells the
Friend that his provocation for writing satire is simply
his "strong antipathy of Good to Bad," he again rises to a
peak similar to the close of *Dialogue I*, this time pro-
voked by the Friend's unfortunate remark on pride:

> *Fr.*   You're strangely proud.
>   *P.*   So proud, I am no Slave:
> 2 So impudent, I own myself no Knave:
>   So odd, my Country's Ruin make me grave.
> 4 Yes, I am proud; I must be proud to see
>   Men not afraid of God, afraid of me:
> 6 Safe from the Bar, the Pulpit, and the Throne,
>   Yet touch'd and sham'd by *Ridicule* alone.
> 8   O sacred Weapon! left for Truth's defense,
>   Sole Dread of Folly, Vice, and Insolence!
> 10 To all but Heav'n-directed hands deny'd,
>   The Muse may give thee, but the Gods must guide.
> 12 Rev'rent I touch thee! but with honest zeal;
>   To rowze the Watchmen of the Public Weal,

14 To Virtue's Work provoke the tardy Hall,
   And goad the Prelate slumb'ring in his Stall.
16   Ye tinsel Insects' whom a Court maintains,
   That counts your Beauties only by your Stains,
18 Spin all your Cobwebs o'er the Eye of Day!
   The Muse's wing shall brush you all away:
20 All his Grace preaches, all his Lordship sings,
   All that makes Saints of Queens, and Gods of Kings,
22 All, all but Truth, drops dead-born from the Press,
   Like the last Gazette, or the last Address.

(II. 204–27)

The antitheses of the first paragraph, which are climaxed by the almost blasphemous one of line 5, are achieved in quite a different manner and have a different kind of effect from those typical of the early poems, or even those of the *Epistle to Burlington*. The second half of each parallel does not suggest or imitate in its syntax the first half of the antithesis; for Pope does not use words that pose antithesis, such as "but," and the pairs of words that make alternatives which we have noted earlier, such as "either–or," "this–that," and so on. In the first line he springs the opening antithesis with the use of "so," and the climactic one in line 5 with the repetition of "afraid." Actually Pope creates a quality of oxymoron rather than pure antithesis; and the lines achieve a linear kind of movement rather than the polyphonic lamination typical of most of his antithetic passages before the *Imitations of Horace*.

The second paragraph qualifies the shocking directness of the first by showing the Satirist in the act of transcending his egotism to take up reverently the God–given instrument. Neither in this paragraph does Pope employ any unusual structure, nor in the last paragraph, except perhaps in its modulation of the lines. Line

19, which could not possibly be any simpler or more direct, puts "All" in action in the three following anaphoral parallels. As "all" is repeated, it acquires increasing intensity until the predicate for the three lines beginning with "All," falls into place in the penultimate line, "drops dead-born from the Press." The design of the whole reflects the rhythm of the idea: the shattering irony of the first paragraph is inspired with an egotism that is justified by the proper use of satire in the second paragraph; and in the third paragraph, satire itself becomes the "muse's Wing," brushing the vice of a corrupt and decadent society from the "Eye of Day."

After a vehement passage which contrasts honor and virtue with flattery, envy and ambition, and which envisions the final triumph of virtue as its incense rises to grateful skies, Pope closes the poem:

> Yes, the last Pen for Freedom let me draw,
> When Truth stands trembling on the edge of Law;
> Here, last of *Britons!* let your Names be read;
> Are none, none living? let me praise the Dead,
> And for that Cause which made your Fathers shine,
> Fall, by the Votes of their degen'rate Line!
>   *Fr.*   Alas! alas! pray end what you began,
> And write next winter more *Essays on Man.*
>
>   (II. 248–55)

Pope's speech has a deliberate, measured intensity: every line except the last contains nine words; and most of the unaccented syllables receive a stronger than usual accent. Pope works here with an inexact antithesis which has a strong metaphoric force: in the first line he draws the sword for a cause which made Britons' fathers shine. The pen of freedom, or rather the sword which the new libel law may force the Satirist to sheathe, is figuratively held

up while he praises the dead. Then the periodic third
couplet throws the climactic verb, "Fall," into the first
position and the antithesis is swept home. Even in his
intensity Pope's grim humor does not desert him, and
the Friend's alarmed impertinence catches the concision
and directness of the piercing satire he disapproves. The
syntax is spare, terse; and the antithetic idea receives a
longer rhythmic sweep than Pope's earlier forms of balanced antithesis could have given it.

The final two passages above, as well as others in the
late poems, illustrate two general principles (to which
there are some exceptions) in Pope's development of his
couplet. First, antithesis is put in lines that do not use
pivotally balanced parallels; and second, ironic recoil of
meaning is developed in a more linear manner and is
more spread out and amplified than earlier. The spring
of Pope's wit has a longer recoil. In an early poem, Pope,
more often than not, laminates the type of irony and
paradox in the passages above by placing witty, antithetic lines throughout the passage, passing to the climax
by a step by step progression, layering the wit by varied
repetition. In the *Epilogue*, antithesis and wit develop
with fewer geometric manifestations of syntax.

Very little that one can say about the dominant couplet styles of the *Pastorals*, the *Essay on Criticism*,
Windsor-Forest, *The Rape of the Lock*, and even the
Essay on Man is true of the *Epilogue*. Perhaps this statement seems misleading, since all of Pope's major poems
bear the unmistakable mark of his concision and grace.
But when the later works are compared with the early
ones, a subtle spectrum of difference appears in any descriptive terms applied to the whole of Pope's work.
There are no couplet norms or dominant stylistic modes

in the *Epilogue* similar to those of the early poems because Pope does not use the same type of structured
norm or dominant style, nor is there a particular structure or mode that occurs frequently enough to enable
Pope to refer to it as a thematic device or *leit motif*.
Structural features which differentiate norm from variation and appear massed together in particular paragraphs
in earlier poems do not occur in the *Epilogue*, for almost
every couplet has a different structure. The most frequent couplet is a closed one of simple and varied structure without antithesis or balance, which forms a contin-
uum of dominant style rather than norm. Most of its
rhymes are neutral; and even when they are not, their
ironies and poetic complications are achieved with an
even simpler and more casual line structure than in the
Epistle to Burlington and the *Epistle to Dr. Arbuthnot*.
The syntax is as simple and varied as colloquial speech,
one should add, of the highest caliber. Pope's irony is as
rich as ever, but the Satirist, and the poet, who wrote the
Epilogue is not the same satirist who wrote the earlier
Moral Essays or the *Epistle to Dr. Arbuthnot*; and the
style of the *Epilogue* expresses this change. It is as if
there is no time left in this poem, not even for the
magnificent play of balance and parallelism.

NOTES

1. The best treatment of Pope's handling of the satiric opponent or
adversary is John M. Aden's "Pope and the Satiric Adversary," *Essential
Articles for the Study of Alexander Pope*, ed. Maynard Mack (Hamden,
Conn.: Archon Books, 1964), pp. 569–90, reprinted from *SEL*, II
(1962).

2. For a more complete discussion of how the dialogue works, see
Aden, above.

10

Conclusion

POPE's different couplet styles in the eight poems of this study depend upon the complex and subtle handling of just two basic features of the couplet—balance and closure. If this seems like an oversimplification, let us remember that balance implies nonbalance, and closure implies the opposite, the open or suspended couplet that is incomplete in meaning. Closure is more frequently a characteristic of the couplet than of the line, since the couplet is more often complete in meaning than the line. Balance is a characteristic either of the line or the couplet; and while Pope frequently balances or parallels one line of the couplet against the other, he more frequently balances one-half of the line against the other half. The handling of balance and parallelism is a correlative of the handling of sentence structure; and it seems a fruitless task to try to determine which comes first, the line and the couplet or the sentence, or which determines the form of the other. They are a *gestalt* and occur together, just as in the greatest works of art form and content are felt to be the same. But one can make, at least, a slight generalization about Pope's handling of the relation between the couplet and the sentence: in his early poems

he shows a tendency to compose in terms of line structure, in the later poems in terms of the sentence. This
does not make a late poem a better poem, necessarily,
than an early one; it makes it a poem with a different
kind of couplet style. One can find couplets in *Windsor-
Forest* and the *Essay on Criticism* that are stiff and
ineffective because of Pope's unresolved tension between
the line and the sentence. The *Rape of the Lock*, however, shows a masterful handling of line composition
when it is fitting that the thought be formed by the line
rather than the sentence—"Or stain her Honour, or her
new Brocade"—and an equally masterful use of the simple, straightforward sentence that we saw Pope use in the
norm couplets of that poem. But from the *Dunciad
Variorum* to the end of his career, Pope's tendency is to
put more emphasis upon the sentence and less upon the
line.

The balanced line is the basic feature of the couplet
upon which Pope based his stylistic developments. Generally he used less balance in the later poems and de-
pended less on zeugma and chiasmus. With less antithetic balance, he used fewer inversions; and if one grants
Pope the same liberty of inversion as is usually given
other poets, his inversions were not frequent in poems
later than the *Essay on Man*. As a result, the continuity
from couplet to couplet grew simpler, less patterned, and
more proselike. The lack of linear, unpatterned, proselike
continuity in early poems is compensated for by closer
binding in the rhymes and by the chiastic interplay of
parallels. I do not mean that the couplets of Pope's early
poems lack continuity, but that it is a different kind from
the continuity of the late poems. In the late poems one
closed couplet follows another with a simple, linear syn-

tax, while brilliance with parallelism gives way to less geometrically witty effects. In the *Rape of the Lock* (1714) Pope used the stricter, more formal kinds of antithetic and parallel balance more brilliantly than he was ever to do later; from *Eloisa to Abelard* (1717) to the end of his career, the sharp and witty structures characteristic of the *Essay on Criticism* and the *Rape of the Lock* are softened, varied, and also less frequent. Pope continued to employ balance and parallelism, but it is not the norm or dominant style of poems, except the *Essay on Man*, later than the *Rape of the Lock*. By the time of the *Dunciad Variorum* in 1728, Pope embodied complex satire in a more direct and proselike syntax than is characteristic of the earlier poems; and though his antithetic parallels are still at work, they are not as closely confined in separate couplets as earlier, and are subordinated to the designs of the enclosing passages.

Balance, with its sharp, symmetrical effects should not be underemphasized in Pope's poetry, nor should it be overemphasized, as it usually is. Geoffrey Tillotson's accurate and persuasive treatment of a single couplet illustrates a typical process of Pope's balance, and tempts one to see this process at work in all of Pope's verse:

> Their [Denham, Waller, Dryden] kind of verbal manipulation was improved on, until in Pope a couplet will often suggest a figure in Euclid, its vowels and consonants, its sense-oppositions and sense-attractions, fitted together like arcs and lines.
>
> > A Fop their Passion, but their Prize a Sot;
> > Alive, ridiculous, and dead, forgot!
>
> A manner such as this keeps the reader's brain active, fetching and carrying. It is a metre for educated people. No meaning is possible for the 'mind' to review, or for

the 'spirit' to kindle at, till the 'brain' has mastered the Euclidean relationships.[1]

Tillotson's statement, one notices, is qualified, and is not meant to apply to the whole of Pope's poetry, but too many readers assume that Pope employs much more balance than he actually does. Pope, in fact, employs Tillotson's Euclidean "elements" throughout his career, but the frequency varies. In almost every poem, Pope varies, contrasts, and often controls his geometric antithesis and balance with verse designs in which the movements and rhythms of the couplets are more fluid and wavelike than his typical balances. When Pope is most successful, the form of the whole poem and its stylistic design control antithetic balance, as in *Windsor-Forest*, while geometric structures with their antithetic relations are transcended and given different perspectives by larger themes than those of particular balanced couplets.

To read Pope is to be concerned with balance and parallelism, but we must not forget that when we deal with balance, no matter how sharp or geometric, we are still dealing with language, not logic or mathematics; and Pope deals in ambiguity like any other poet, as William Empson has shown.[2] A too close identification of Pope's poetry with balance and parallelism harms the full appreciation of his verse. How does one describe, or account for the character of the following passage, one of Pope's most famous "portraits," and what is the nature of the art which creates these lines?

> Peace to all such! but were there One whose fires
> True Genius kindles, and fair Fame inspires,
> Blest with each Talent and each Art to please,
> And born to write, converse, and live with ease:
> Shou'd such a man, too fond to rule alone,

Bear, like the *Turk*, no brother near the throne,
View him with scornful, yet with jealous eyes,
And hate for Arts that caus'd himself to rise;
Damn with faint praise, assent with civil leer,
And without sneering, teach the rest to sneer;
Willing to wound, and yet afraid to strike,
Just hint a fault, and hesitate dislike;
Alike reserv'd to blame, or to commend,
A tim'rous foe, and a suspicious friend,
Dreading ev'n fools, by Flatterers besieg'd,
And so obliging that he ne'er oblig'd;
Like *Cato*, give his little Senate laws,
And sit attentive to his own applause;
While Wits and Templers ev'ry sentence raise,
And wonder with a foolish face of praise.
Who but must laugh, if such a man there be?
Who would not weep, if *Atticus* were he!
                              (*Epistle to Dr. Arbuthnot*, 193–214)

It does not matter that this is a satiric picture of Joseph Addison: Atticus is simply a character in the poem. Pope starts building him up in the first four lines, then the style, like the crest of a wave, sweeps Atticus down, and by the end, the reader's complicated appreciation of the wit and satire is touched with regret. The passage is a masterpiece of the art of negation. Atticus is given, not solid worth or integrity, but merely possibility, and even this is destroyed by the sharp, exact balances which create, strangely enough, an uncertainty, and cold, mean ambiguity in the character. It is true that these parallels can suggest geometric relationships; but if one attempted to number their terms according to some kind of chiastic order, or to draw arcs and lines showing their exact relationships, one would certainly go mad from their subtle complications.

Surely Pope's technique in this passage and in many

others like it should suggest something more than the usual platitudes about his grace, precision, or sharpness. Comparisons of one art with another are almost never satisfactory, but perhaps it will help here to suggest the following viewpoint. The technique of parallelism in the Atticus portrait resembles one often used by twentieth century artists (Picasso or Braque among the larger figures) to represent several views of the same object at the same time, as in some styles of Cubism in which the angles and planes of one surface are superimposed upon and radiate from those of another surface. For instance, in some of Picasso's earlier Cubistic paintings, the face of a subject or the surfaces of an object are displaced and refracted into different lines, planes and angles, yet the subject, seen from a multiple perspective, holds all in a central focus. The character of Atticus has several ambiguous and negative facets, and Pope's antithetic parallels suggest the transparent surfaces of a Cubistic painting beneath which gleam tilted planes and lines, all of which are refracted by Atticus' character. As Pope has sketched him, Atticus is a fitter subject for Picasso or Braque than for Reynolds, Gainsborough, or even Hogarth.

Since Pope decreased his use of balance, and increased, very slightly, his use of open couplets, it is logical to suppose that he augmented his use of enjambment or run-on lines. He did, very slightly, but not because of any one single or obvious reason. The second book of the *Dunciad Variorum*, which describes the heroic games, has a relatively high percentage of run-on lines: 17 percent of the couplets employ a run-on line, which does not mean that 17 percent of the lines are run-on, but that actually 8.5 percent of the lines are run-on. The run-on's help the sonorous diction emphasize the mock-heroic elements in the ludicrous and ugly content. The highest percentage of run-on's, however, 18 percent, occurs in the first dialogue of the *Epilogue to the Satires,* a different kind of poem from the second book of the *Dunciad.* In the first dialogue, they reflect quick, conversational give-and-take and a colloquial tone. Paradoxically, there are twice as many run-on's in *Dialogue I* as there are in *Dialogue II;* the first is 90 lines shorter, yet the two poems are similar in style and tone. The reason for this apparent inconsistency is that the first reflects the thrusts of actual conversation. The Friend attempts a kind of too familiar and condescending persuasion, and Pope leads him on sarcastically, in like manner, to trap and expose him. In *Dialogue II,* however, Pope has a different Friend or Adversary; the exchanges grow more vehement, are less persuasive and informal, so the couplets are closed, and, on the whole, more emphatic. Thus a concrete reason in a particular work always accounts for the number of run-on lines. One might expect Pope to use a great many run-on's in Book IV of the *Dunciad* to express the sublimity of his vision of Dulness' power and divinity, but he uses other methods. About 12 percent of the couplets of the fourth book have a run-on line; the *Essay on Criticism* has 9 percent, and surprisingly, the *Epistle to Dr. Arbuthnot* has just 7 percent. What this indicates is that Pope uses run-on lines for various effects, and one can make no generalization about their purpose or effect in the whole of Pope's poetry, but only in particular poems and passages.

When one examines Pope's use of open couplets (a couplet incomplete in meaning), the mere quantitative and chronological results are likewise capricious. The number and kinds of open couplets are integrally related to the length and structure of the sentence, but the structure and design of the couplets are not the same thing as the structure and design of the sentence. The length and structure of the sentence "coexists" with the structure of the couplet and with its openness or closure: a long sentence with parallel subordinate clauses will have open or suspended lines or couplets; but meter, rhyme, the frequent presence of balance, and the tendency of the couplets to vertical binding, force upon the incomplete couplet a power of identity and a complexity that it does not have as a sentence or sentence part. Poetically and metrically, the open or incomplete couplet is more than a sentence part, and the closed couplet more than a sentence. The sentence, as well as its parts, is complicated and crystallized in the line or the couplet because of structure, rhyme, and sound. By itself, the amount of openness or closure does not tell us much about Pope's couplet art, because the effect of openness and closure, and of sentence form and length, changes and varies from poem to poem.

To illustrate the nature of openness and closure, here is a passage from *Windsor-Forest* (1712) describing the contemplative man:

> He gathers Health from Herbs the Forest yields,
> And of their fragrant Physick spoils the Fields:
> With Chymic Art exalts the Min'ral Pow'rs,
> And draws the Aromatick Souls of Flow'rs.
> Now marks the Course of rolling Orbs on high;
> O'er figur'd Worlds now travels with his Eye.
> Of ancient Writ unlocks the learned Store,
> Consults the Dead, and lives past Ages o'er.
> Or wandring thoughtful in the silent Wood,
> Attends the Duties of the Wise and Good,
> T'observe a Mean, be to himself a Friend,
> To follow Nature, and regard his End.   (241–52)

It is unfair to take a weak passage from a good poem, but the sentence form and line structure of this passage illustrates a basic type of open couplet structure. The lines are composed, despite Pope's punctuation, of one sentence, and after the subject "He" in the first line, the lines are merely a series of verb phrases which are predicates. As a contrast, here is a twelve-line passage from *The Second Epistle of the Second Book of Horace* (1737):

> Yes, Sir, how small soever be my heap,
> 2 A part I will enjoy, as well as keep.
> My Heir may sigh, and think it want of Grace
> 4 A man so poor wou'd live without a *Place:*
> But sure no Statute in his favour says,
> 6 How free, or frugal, I shall pass my days:
> I, who at some times spend, at others spare,
> 8 Divided between Carelessness and Care.
> 'Tis one thing madly to disperse my store,
> 10 Another, not to heed to treasure more;
> Glad, like a Boy, to snatch the first good day,
> 12 And pleas'd, if sordid Want be far away.　(284–95)

There are four sentences here: lines 1–2, 3–4, 5–8, 9–12. Pope uses his typical antithesis which is achieved, however, with a more direct and naturally ordered syntax than in early works. But the distinctive mark of the passage compared with the lines from *Windsor-Forest* is that its lines seem more open and suspended, freer than the rigid lines of the first passage. In the second passage, line structure, sentence structure, and the methods of continuity and reference are looser, less explicit. In lines 7–8, the completion of the sentence begun in line 5 is accomplished with a grammatical and structural freedom that Pope did not risk in the *Pastorals* and *Windsor-Forest*. Without attempting a more detailed analysis of the diction and rhythm of the two passages at this point, it is perhaps clear enough that the differences between the two passages depend upon Pope's different handling of all the elements of the couplet, as well as upon a basic difference of theme, tone, and point of view. The two passages show that openness and closure are not really clearcut, well-defined concepts that can be applied to the whole of Pope's verse. The first passage is a simple and very explicit sentence of twelve lines, but the short sentences of the second passage, especially the last two, are more complex in structure and subtle in transition. To compare and evaluate the effects of openness or closure, therefore, means that other elements of the couplet must be evaluated also, and openness or closure has no significance except in particular passages and poems.

There is a slight increase in the percentage of open couplets from the *Pastorals* to the *Epilogue to the Satires,* but the increase does not follow a consistent pattern. The *Pastorals* have the fewest open couplets, 10 percent, and consequently the highest proportion of closed couplets. From the *Pastorals* on, the range of openness is about 20 to 30 percent for most of the poems in this study. The first book of the *Dunciad* of 1743 has the most, 35 percent; but the *Epilogue* has only 20 percent compared with 19 percent for the *Essay on Criticism,* and 22 percent for the *Rape of the Lock.* There is, however, an important difference in the manner in which the closure is managed, which really amounts to a difference in line structure. The open couplets of the early poems are often created by a strict parallelism and balance which neatly compounds subjects, verbs, and predicates. Clauses and phrases are made sharply discrete because of the grammatical and syntactic division of the line; and frequently in these poems, Pope uses a series of layered phrases or clauses to sustain the openness which means to postpone the completion of meaning. The couplets of the late poems, on the other hand, are more dramatic and conversational, and sentence form and line structure is not as much governed by the division of the line into halves or by the couplet into two compound lines. In the late poems lines which begin with "and," as compared with lines beginning with "and" in the early poems, do not as often compound subject, predicate, or object, but make a new predication or turn the sentence in a different direction. If Pope, therefore, gives up in the late poems some of the effects depending upon laminated line structure and the brilliant play with rhymes depending on parallelism, he gains in conversational tone and rapid movement.

Rhyme, a main factor of all the preceding parts and characteristics of Pope's couplet, is determined by none of them, but influenced by all. A major pattern in Pope's rhymes is the one isolated and discussed by Wimsatt that has already been noted and used several times in this study: that Pope rhymes words whose effect depends upon some clever or shocking disparity or twist of the difference of meaning between the words, the alogical relation of the rhyme words creating a humorous or ironic resemblance, or difference, between the rhyme words which is emphasized by Pope's rhyming of different parts of speech; and that the difference of the rhyme words gains in richness because of the tendency of Pope's couplets to parallel structure.[3] Even this pattern (as I have tried to demonstrate), is not a constant one, but is shifting and multivalent, and by no means describes or defines the whole range of Pope's rhyming technique.

Pope's rhyming, like his balance and parallelism, deceives one to make the faulty generalization, even so fine a scholar as Tillotson:

> All through his work Pope seems to have preferred a verb for at least one of the rime-words in a couplet. This was a means of attaining a full stress for the rime. A verb at the end of the first line is often followed by its object in the next line. This provided the couplet with bipartite unity instead of with unified duality.[4]

But this merely seems to be true because of some striking instances. It would be more accurate to say that Pope preferred a noun, instead of a verb, for at least one of the rhyme words in a couplet; and it is not true that "a verb at the end of the first line is often followed by its object in the next line." What actually happens is that when the first line ends with a verb, it will more often be followed with some other completion than its object in the next line, or it will be an intransitive verb. In a poem or passage with considerable inversion, the verb which ends the first line has its object or other completion in the first line also. The grammatical and formal principle of Pope's rhymes, if there is one, or several, is much more elusive than Tillotson makes it appear. Pope rhymes nouns more than any other part of speech, with verbs as a not-so-close second, but he rhymes any part of speech in a variety of structures, especially in the *Dunciad* and later poems. Since rhyming bears a crucial relation to line structure and consequently to balance, and since Pope decreased his use of balance and relied less on oppositions of structure, his rhyming in later poems grew structually straighter and more natural. As a result, he rhymes slightly fewer verbs because of less inversion, and more words which are considered weak rhymes such as adverbs and adjectives. His rhyming, therefore, is less emphatic in the later works, for he relies less upon sharp contrasts of structure and meaning. But he gives up nothing of his irony, nor of his poetry; his art is quieter and one must listen more closely.

Pope's couplet norm for all his works, which is nothing more than a closed, end-stopped couplet of great economy and concision with caesura in one line, not two, and without balanced antithesis, is constantly varied, until the *Epistle to Dr. Arbuthnot*, by the couplet with a balanced line. The balanced line, particularly the antithetic balance, sets up a tension against the linear forward movement of exposition and narration. If the couplets keep closing and balancing without forward movement of the meaning, the result is tricky, shuttling, see-sawing motion that quickly grows monotonous in spite of other interesting qualities. This sometimes happens in the *Essay on Man* after Epistle I, and to a slighter extent in the third part of the *Essay on Criticism*. In both poems the aphoristic and exhortative couplets come a little too frequently. On the other hand, Pope is more successful when he achieves a relentless forward movement of the narration or exposition, and when he does not concentrate too long upon antithetic balance and the Latin and French types of syntax that sometimes accompany it, especially in the poems up to 1717. Perhaps the *Essay on Man* would strike more readers as convincing and consistent had Pope used more of the rugged, irregular, proselike couplets characteristic of the *Dunciad* and the *Imitations of Horace* and less of the antithesis characteristic of the *Essay on Criticism*. The *Rape of the Lock* is in many ways the most successful of Pope's poems and serves usefully as a touchstone or norm of Pope's art. It is graceful, and for couplet poetry, swift. Pope's witty rhymes and balances are always subservient to theme and to the forward movement of the story. Striking couplets never seem ornamental or digressive. Pope's methods all work in harmony and his incisive balance and parallelism function as a brilliant analytic technique which throws varying perspectives upon the story, idea, or theme as it moves along. As Belinda whirls through her day, Pope's balance, chiasmus, and zeugma enable the reader to see her from several, almost simultaneous, viewpoints while Pope's narrative skill and linear couplet norm move the story rapidly. This symbiotic relation between movement and stylistic variety is not a formula or scheme, but rather an organic pattern that Pope uses successfully in all his best poems. But Pope, as we have seen, does not work merely with the couplet of balanced antithesis or balanced parallelism which is varied regularly with the neutral or unpatterned couplet. In all his best poems he gives individual designs to passages and paragraphs— what can be called rhythms of structure—to increase the scope and variety of his style beyond that of any other couplet poet, including Dryden.

All of Pope's work seems to be, as G. Wilson Knight claims, "a single organic whole."[5] The fact that all of his poetry that really matters is written in the heroic couplet is a reflection of this organic whole, but it does not determine it. Pope's imaginative vision of his world and his conception of its forms of order is the basis of his poetry; and it is doubtless true that the couplet, especially with its varied and subtle balance and parallelism, expresses Pope's conception of his world in the profoundest sense. Pope saw the world as a vast and complex system of balanced oppositions, of harmonious strife founded upon the law of *concordia discors* and the Great Chain of Being. This system worked ultimately for good, but its workings were complicated by the given conditions of the capricious human personality (ruling passion) and the corrupt human will. In its use of balanced antithesis Pope's couplet expresses this system of oppositions and tensions, but in no schematized or simple way; for his conception of his world and his interpretation and criticism of life is differently expressed and variously focused and represented in different works. We must not forget too, that harmony and agreement is a part of Pope's system of antithetic relationships and must also be expressed. Pope's total style, like his total framework of meaning, represents a tension between concord and discord, or, on a concrete level of style, between consonant parallelism and dissonant antithesis.

This tension in Pope's verse, expressive of his poetic conception of his world, is the abstract and metaphysical pattern to which particular poems are related. But if we make our interpretation of the poem wholly dependent upon Pope's total scheme of meaning or view of his world, the poem becomes too much the illustration of an abstraction; it loses its individuality and sense of identity and becomes a dialectic, a diagram, or an equation. Because Pope found the rigid requirements of the couplet form sufficient to express all he wanted to say, and because there is a general resemblance of couplet style and structure between any two of his poems, we are perhaps tempted to see Pope's poetic world as more tightly unified than it really may be. But Pope had not only a coherent set of assumptions, a philosophic outlook upon man, society, and metaphysical order that he consistently and variously articulated in his poems. He had a sensibility and personality which gave a personal texture and color to the details of his poetry. Although his use of description and of the materials of everyday life is often thematic, a use not primarily for the sake of the things themselves, yet his expression of the life of the senses, of the quality and character of concrete things, is always accurate, appreciative, and uniquely his own. Pope brought also to the writing of each poem a sense of authorial character and role that creates a point of view and sense of involvement, which, as we have seen, is a dynamic influence upon his style. Each of Pope's major poems, while related to, and a part of, the organic whole of his work, expresses in varying degrees, and in a variety of modes, not only the involvement of the poem in this whole and its relation to it, but its own individual character and poetic integrity.

The end of this study has returned to its beginning. It grants—and has pointed out—the wholeness and unity of Pope's work; but its main point is the same one with which it began: that Pope's couplet style in each major poem shapes and expresses that one poem and no other.

NOTES

1. *Augustan Studies*, pp. 14–15.

2. *Seven Types of Ambiguity* (Cleveland: The World Publishing Company, 1964), pp. 82–86, 169–72, and many other places in this work. See also Empson's treatment of wit in the *Essay on Criticism* in *The Structure of Complex Words* (Norfolk, Conn.: New Directions), pp. 84–100.

3. *The Verbal Icon*, pp. 153–66, *passim*.

4. *On the Poetry of Pope*, p. 124.

5. *Laureate of Peace* (London: Routledge, 1955), p. 5.

Index